日本の紙遊び

ORIGAMI−TSUTSUMI

希夢工房　編・著

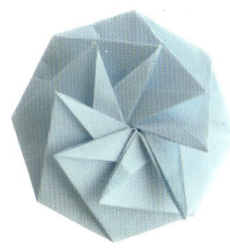

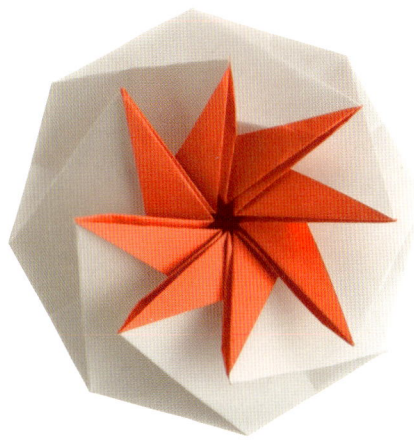

平和を願って鶴を折ります
健康を願って鶴を折ります
夢の実現の為に、エールが
千羽の鶴になります
ありがとうの言葉が
千羽の鶴になります
千羽の鶴を折ることは
祈りのかたちです
希望のかたちです

Folding cranes for peace
Folding cranes for health

Wishes are to be granted
Cranes are cheers
Cranes are gratitudes
Folding thousand cranes is
a form of pray
a form of hope

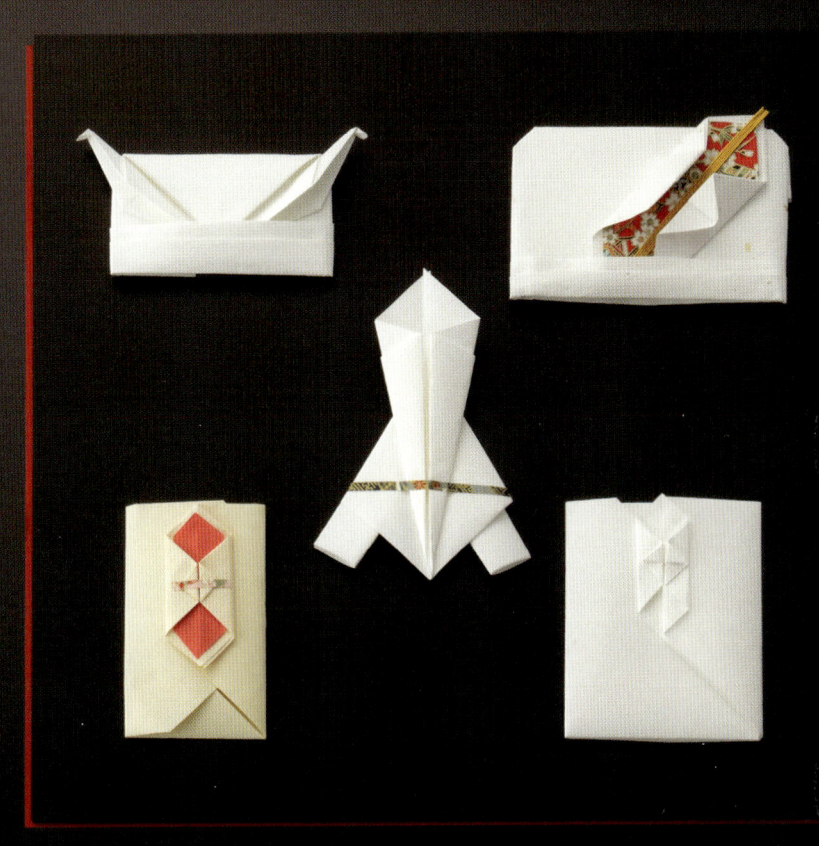

Japan has the conventional practice of enshrining and worshiping eight million gods. It can be found in the form of customs and manners of placing or wrapping offerings to the gods in paper.
This may be peculiar to the Japanese culture.
"Kami", or "gami" of Origami, the Japanese word for paper, is a homonym for gods.
Wrapping offerings in paper is to purify them, as typically found in the divine service.

古来より日本人は、八百よろずの神々を祀り拝むという習慣がありました。神への供え物を、紙に敷く、紙で包むことで礼法作法の形に表しました。
これは日本独特の文化と思われます。
植物の葉や布ではなく植物からできた紙は、神と重なります。
捧げものをするとき紙に包むことで清める意味もあり、神事に使われてきました。

A folded crane is a form of celebration.

折鶴は
幸せな祝いの形です

Japan has the culture of Orikata, folding forms of paper wrapping.
This wrapping culture stems from the Japanese aesthetic sense that presenting goods as exposed is discourtesy. It has been carried out up to now.
A variety of the basic rules of paper wrapping are observed in a pure white wedding garment.

日本には、和紙を折って物を包む「折形」の文化があります。物を直接渡す、直接受けるという事は、失礼にあたるとする日本人の美意識から生まれた包む文化は、今日迄伝えられてきました。
白無垢の花嫁衣装には、和紙で物を包む基本の決まり事が多く表されています。

お嫁さんから
御先祖様へのお土産
御線香を供え
子孫繁栄をお願いします

Offerings to the ancestors by a bride
Wishing prosperity of the descendants,
incense sticks are offered.

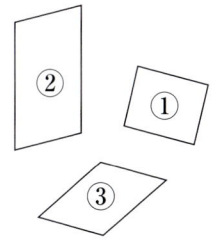

結婚式で使用
① お客様へのメッセージカード立て
② 招待状入れ
③ お干菓子 お昆布 寸志入れ（金封）

At the wedding ceremony
① Message card holder for the guest
② Envelope for the invitation
③ Package for dry confectionery, dry seaweed, a small money

胡麻包み　Package of sesame

Package of little items

Sesame
Hot pepper
Medicine
Plant seeds

小物入れ
胡麻
唐辛子
薬
植物の種

日本の五節句

一月七日　人日の節句―七草
三月三日　桃の節句―ひな祭り
五月五日　端午の節句―こいのぼり
七月七日　七夕の節句―星祭り
九月九日　重陽の節句―菊の節句

The five seasonal festivals in Japan

January 7　Jinjitsu-no-sekku – Nanakusa
　　　　　　<Seven spring herbs>
March 3　　Momo-no-sekku – Hina-matsuri
　　　　　　<Hina festival>
May 5　　　Tango-no-sekku – Koi-nobori
　　　　　　<Carp streamers>
July 7　　　Shichiseki-no-sekku – Hoshi-matsuri
　　　　　　<Star festival>
September 9　Chouyou-no-sekku – Kiku-no-sekku
　　　　　　<Chrysanthemum festival>

Hina festival

私のひな祭り

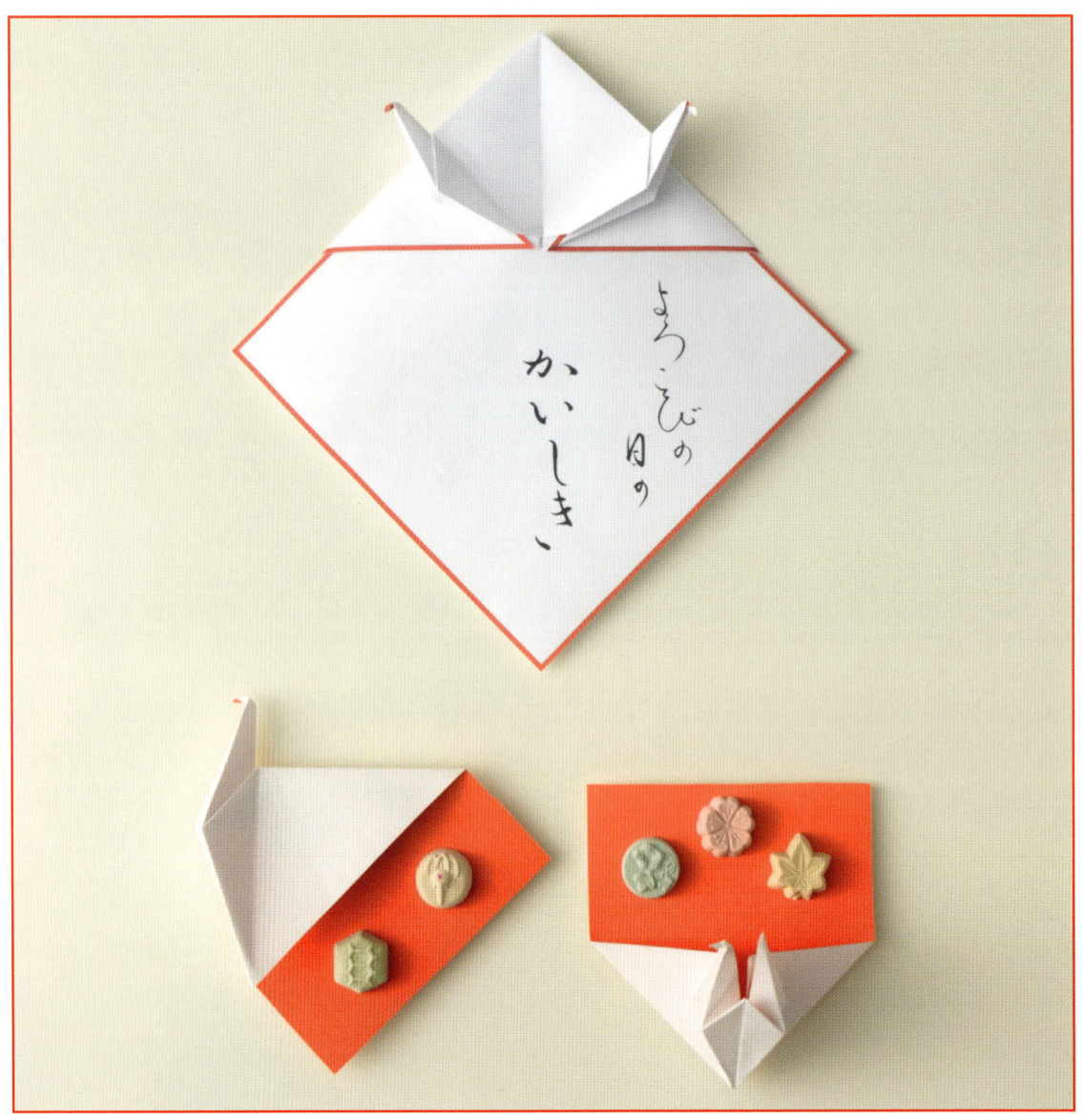

端午の節句
こどもの日
子供達の健やかな
成長を願う日

Tango-no-sekku

Wishing for children's healthy growth

Kanreki celebration

There used to be the custom to give Chanchanko (a red vest) as a gift on someone's 60th birthday. After the custom, a package for a money envelope is made in the form of Chanchanko. "Kanreki" literally means "return to the calendar" based on the Chinese calendar of a sixty-year cycle.

還暦のお祝い

還暦には長寿と健康を願って"赤いちゃんちゃんこ"を贈る風習がありました。これは、その風習にちなんでちゃんちゃんこの形に折った金封入れです。

Money envelope inserted in the back

背中に金封を入れます

昭和の中頃迄、"おめざ"という習慣がありました。「明日の朝はおめざがあるから」と早くに寝かされた翌朝、早暁の薄明かりの中、枕元に白い紙の包みを見つけると、どきどきわくわくしたものです。半紙の中は、おままごとのお道具であったり、飴や金平糖のおひねり、あるいは芝居見物の土産が包んでありました。

Up to the mid-Showa era (1960's), there was a practice called "Omeza" (wake-up gifts). Parents place gifts by children's pillows. The children get excited to find them wrapped in white paper in the dim light of dawn. In packages, they find such gifts as playing house kits and candies.

Octagonal Tatou
(folding case)

八角のたとう

黒文字入れ

Kuromoji case
(Kuromoji: a special pick
for fresh Japanese sweets)

鶴箸袋

Crane chopstick case

Incense envelope

薫香包み

As well as flowers, incense is offered to the Shinto's gods and Buddha.
Also, incense can be used in a various way such as to purify the room and to perfume cloths by burning it. When offered, or presented as a gift, incense is packaged in the Tatou folding form.

神仏には花と同じように、薫香のお供えをします。
その他、室内を清める、衣服に焚きしめると多様に用いられます。香を奉納したり、贈ったりする為にも、たとう折が使われてきました。

純白の和紙に品物又はお金を包み、贈り物としてきました。四季、節句等に合わせて贈る中身によって包みの形も変わり、贈り手、受け手どちらも心が和らぎます。

何らかのお手伝いに来て頂いた方に、さしあげる手土産の用意の無い時は、表書きに「お茶菓子」「虫養い」「お車代」と書き、応じた金額を包みます。お金もこんな表書きの衣裳を着ると、受け手の気持ちが和みます。お金を頂くのではなく、「お茶でも飲んで下さい」の声が届き、心からありがとうが言える関係になると思います。

※虫養い――おなかの虫（すき）を一時養う（おさえる）こと

The form of packages varies on occasions. Both the giver and the receiver appreciate its variety. In return for some help, the respectable amount of money is wrapped in paper addressed as "tea cakes", "Mushi Yashinai" or "taxi fare" on the front. Under such addresses, people can accept and appreciate the giver's considerations in a casual manner.
Mushi Yashinai (literally, feeding growling stomach bug) means a temporary relief of emptiness.

Shirt シャツ

成人式
20-year old

二十歳になったお祝いをする国民の式典。

就職
New job

就職は社会人となるスタートのお祝いです。

結婚
Marriage

人生最大の慶び事です。お祝いをする方もされる方も幸せな形を表すように、心を込めて…。
結婚する二人からは感謝の気持ちをお伝えする心を忘れずに。

出産
Childbirth

赤ちゃんの誕生と、出産をした事をお祝いします。

新築
転居
New home

新しい生活がスタートするお祝いです。

還暦
Kanreki (60-year-old)

満60歳になると干支が一巡して生まれた時と同じ干支になります。
これを「暦が還った」という意味で還暦と呼びます。
これから先の長寿を願ってお祝いします。

長寿祝い Longevity	かんれき 還暦 Kanreki	こき 古希（古稀） Koki	きじゅ 喜寿 Kiju	さんじゅ 傘寿 Sanju	べいじゅ 米寿 Beiju	そつじゅ 卒寿 Sotsuju	はくじゅ 白寿 Hakuju	ももじゅ 百寿 きじゅ・ももが（紀寿・百賀） Momoju
数え年	60歳	70歳	77歳	80歳	88歳	90歳	99歳	100歳

おめでとう ありがとうの 記念日
Celebratory occasions

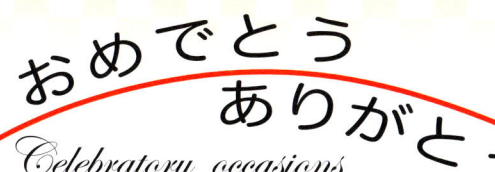

初節句
First seasonal festival

赤ちゃんが生まれてから、初めてのお節句。
祖父母・親族・友人をお招きして、健やかな成長と厄除けの意味を込めて
お祝いをする日本の風習です。

女の子は３月３日　桃の節句
　　　　　　　　　　（桃の花と雛人形を飾って祝います。）

男の子は５月５日　端午の節句
　　　　　　　　　　（邪気を払うと伝えられる菖蒲を飾り、
　　　　　　　　　　葉を入れた菖蒲湯に入ります。）

> お祝いを頂いた方には柏餅、お赤飯等をお返しします。

七五三
7, 5, 3-year old

男の子は満３歳と５歳、女の子は満３歳と７歳の１１月１５日前後に
健やかな成長を願って神社や氏神様に詣で、厄払いをします。

お参りのあと、晴れ着を着て祖父母や親しい方々をお訪ねし、
今日迄の成長の姿を見て頂きます。
子供を迎える方は、おもちゃ、お菓子を用意します。

用意の無い時は、のし袋に　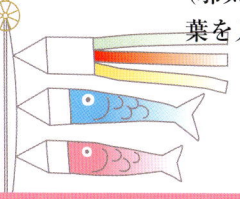　と書いて相当するお金を包み、
渡します。

> この時の内祝いは、お赤飯、又は金封共に下の名前は子供の名前にします。

就学
School enrolment

子供、孫のお祝いとして、お祝い金を渡す事が多く、
本、腕時計、鞄等もお祝い品として贈ります。

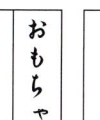

> この時の内祝いは、お赤飯、又は金封。共に下の名前は子供の名前にします。

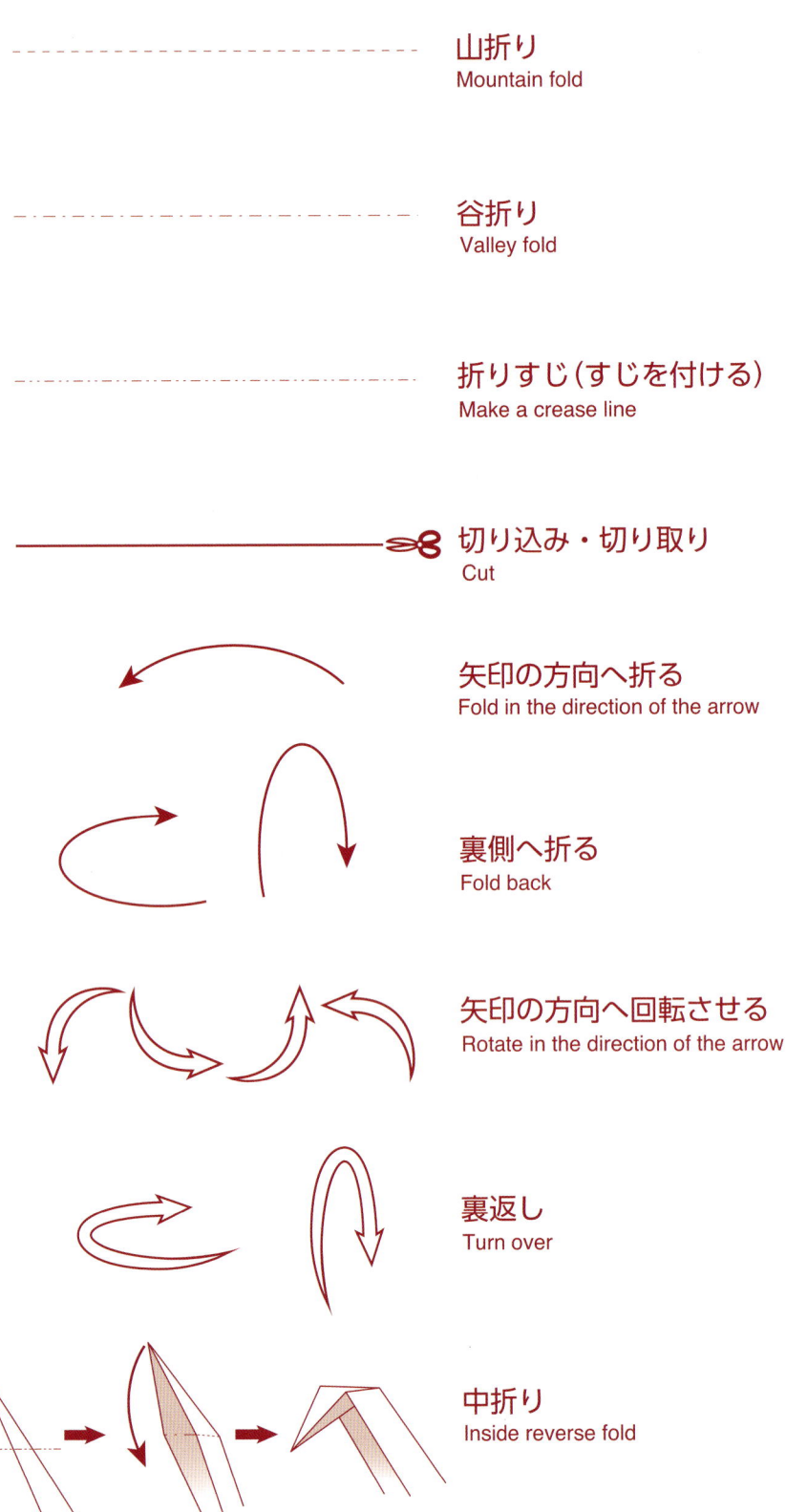

基本の折り方 Basic folding techniques

山折り
Mountain fold

谷折り
Valley fold

折りすじ（すじを付ける）
Make a crease line

切り込み・切り取り
Cut

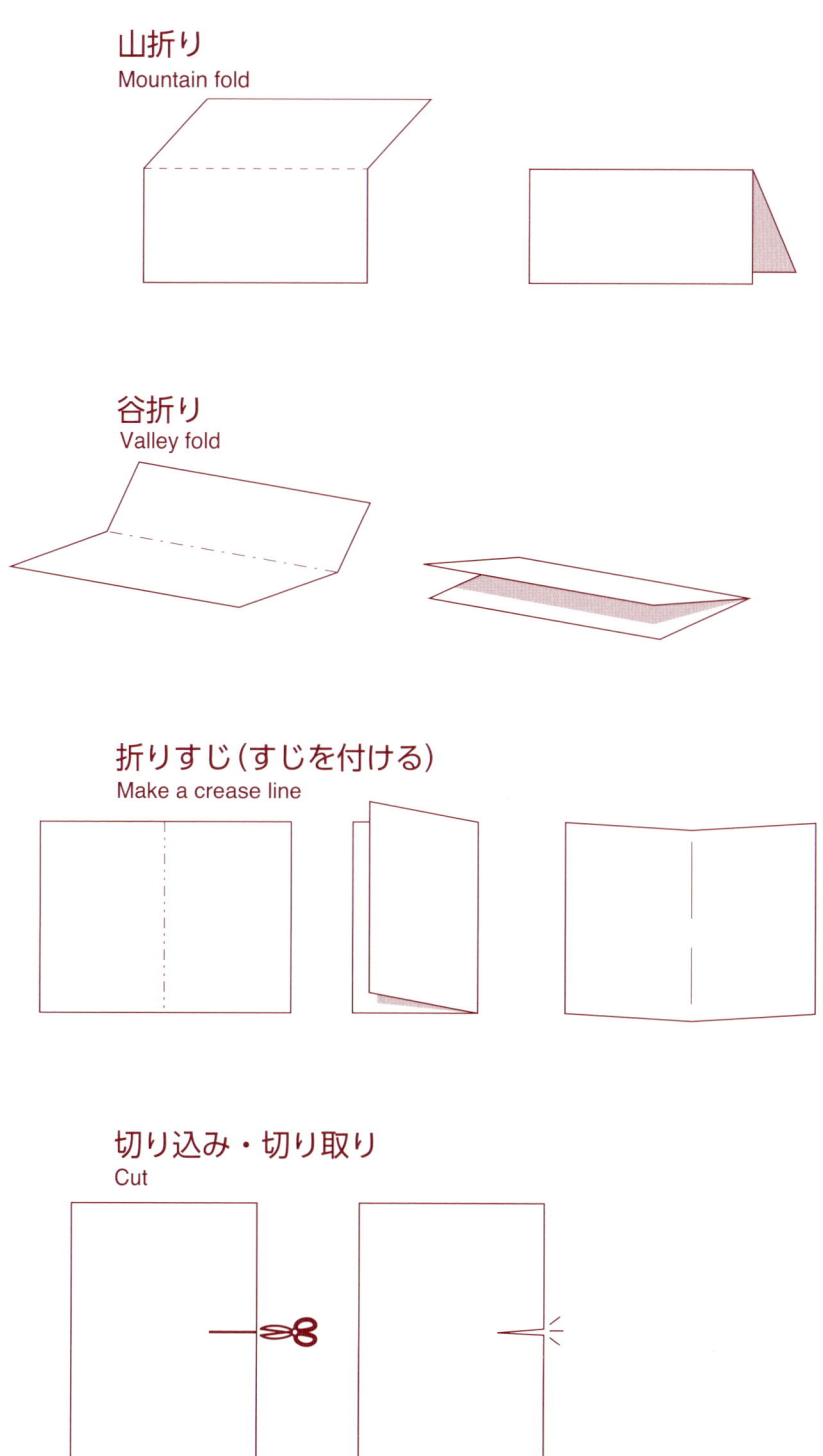

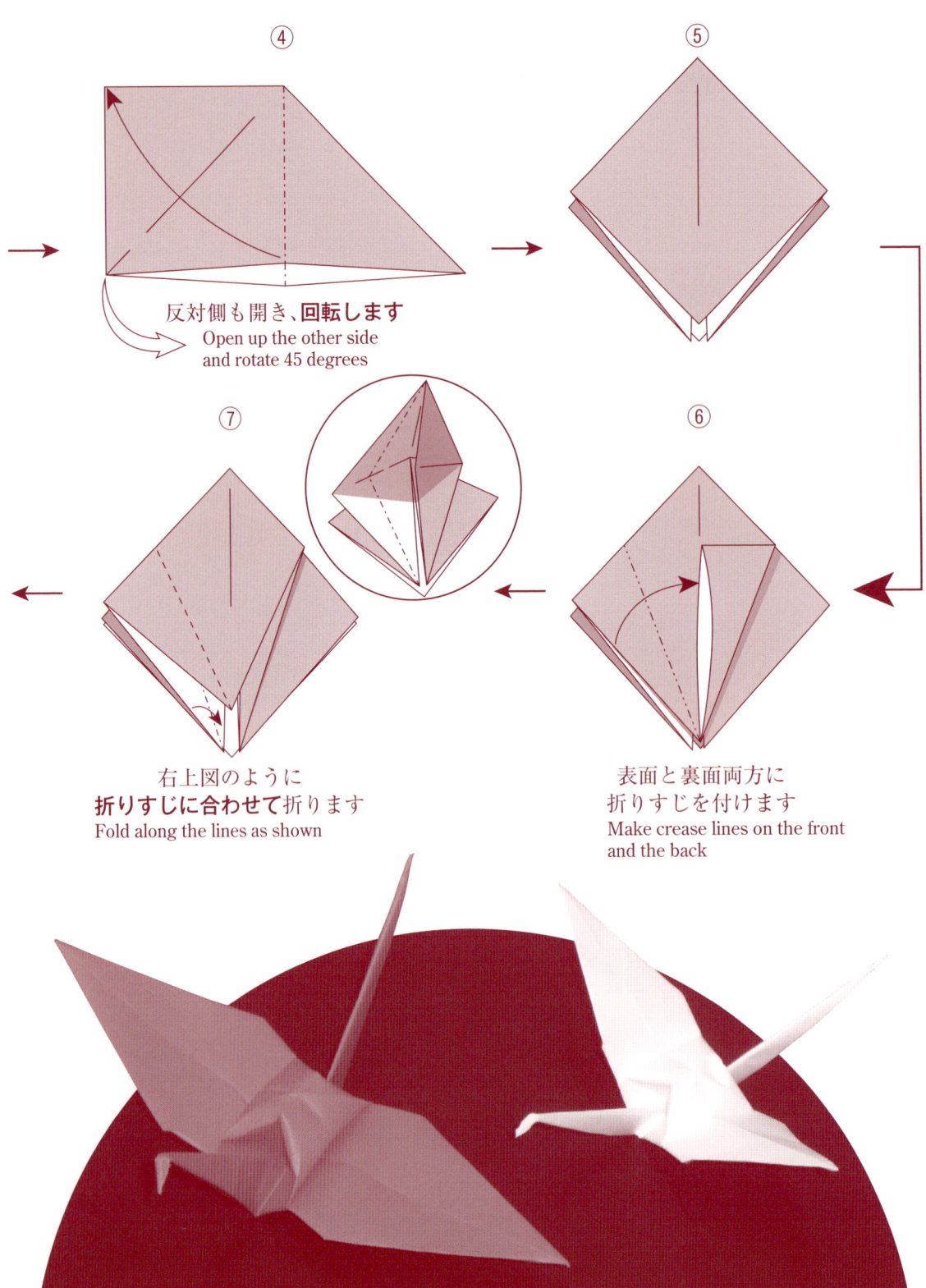

34

基本の鶴を折りましょう! Let's make an authentic crane

2-3,6ページ参照

① ② ③ 開きます Open up

⑪ ⑩ ⑨ ⑧ 表・裏とも上に折ります Fold up on the both sides

中折りで上へ折ります Inside reverse fold up

表・裏とも中心線に合わせて折ります Fold along the center line on the both sides

中折りにします Inside reverse fold

⑫ ⑬ 頭 Head 尾 Tail

頭は小さく折りますと首が長く見えます Fold the head small so that the neck looks long

⑭ 羽を広げます Pull the wings apart

35

④ 折りすじを付けたら元に戻します
Unfold

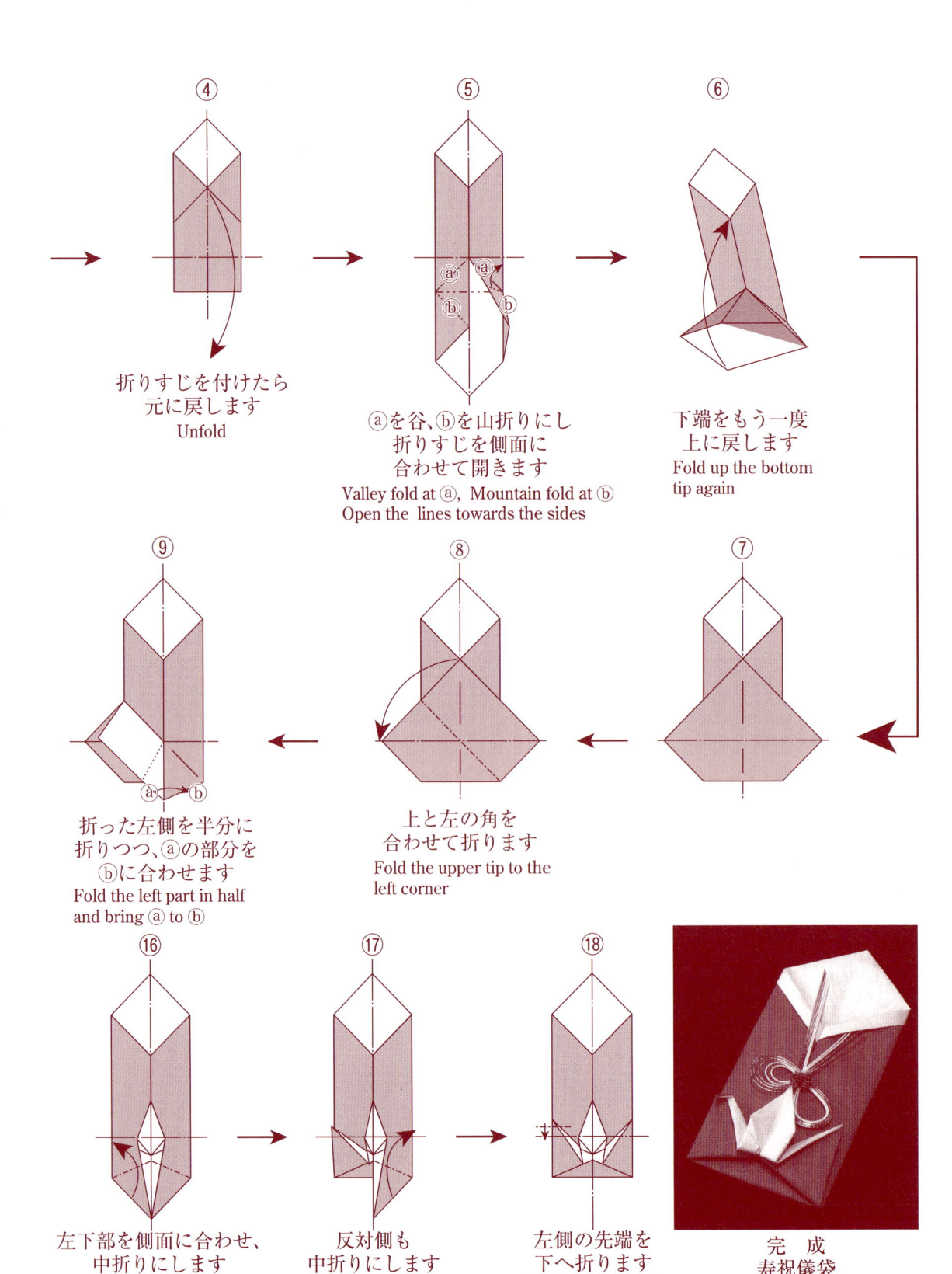

⑤ ⓐを谷、ⓑを山折りにし折りすじを側面に合わせて開きます
Valley fold at ⓐ, Mountain fold at ⓑ
Open the lines towards the sides

⑥ 下端をもう一度上に戻します
Fold up the bottom tip again

⑦

⑧ 上と左の角を合わせて折ります
Fold the upper tip to the left corner

⑨ 折った左側を半分に折りつつ、ⓐの部分をⓑに合わせます
Fold the left part in half and bring ⓐ to ⓑ

⑯ 左下部を側面に合わせ、中折りにします
Inside reverse fold the left bottom part to the side

⑰ 反対側も中折りにします
Inside reverse fold on the other side

⑱ 左側の先端を下へ折ります
Inside reverse fold down the left tip

完成
寿祝儀袋
Completed

36

寿祝儀袋 Celebratory envelope

8ページ参照

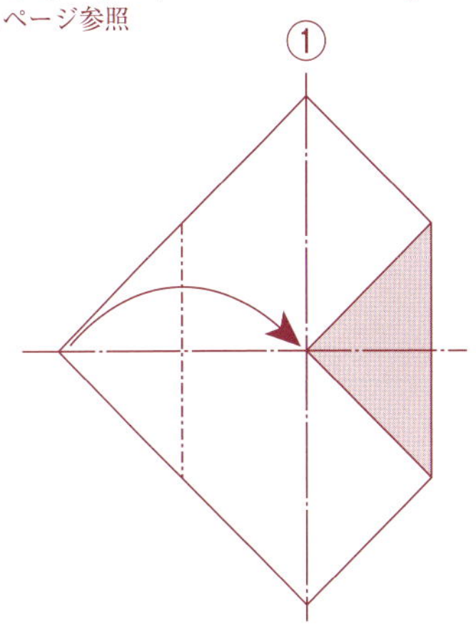

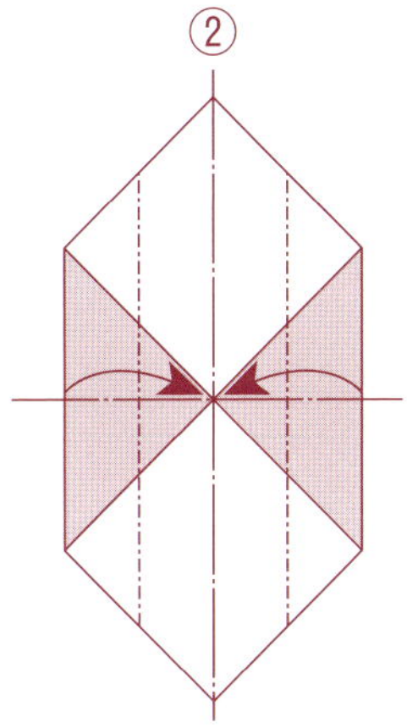

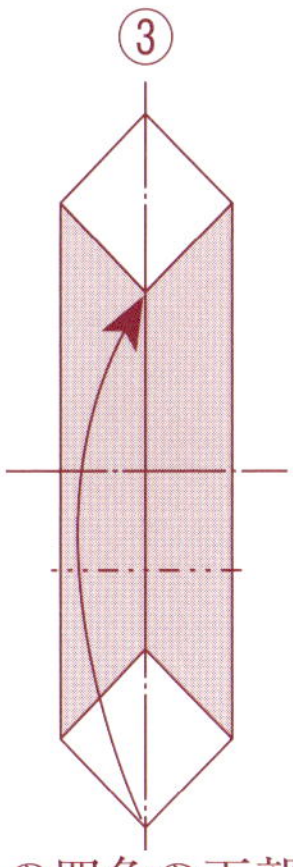

① ② ③

下の先端を上の四角の下部分に合わせて、**折りすじ**を付けます
Bring the bottom tip to the corner of the upper square to make a crease line

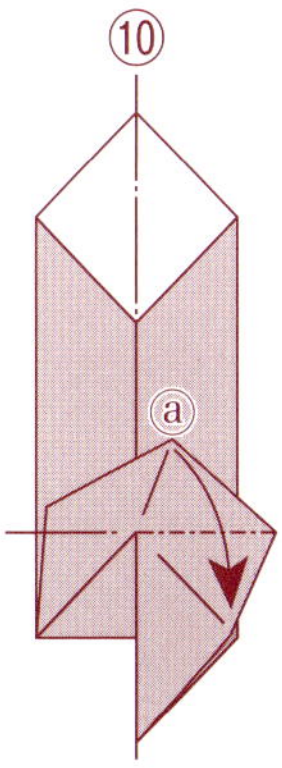

⑫ ⑪ ⑩

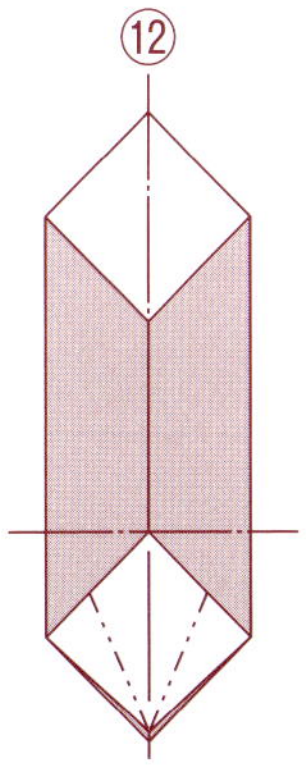

両側に**折りすじ**を付けます
Make crease lines on the both sides

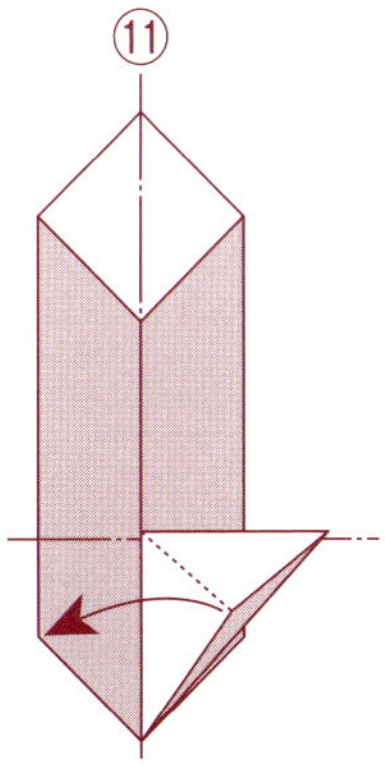

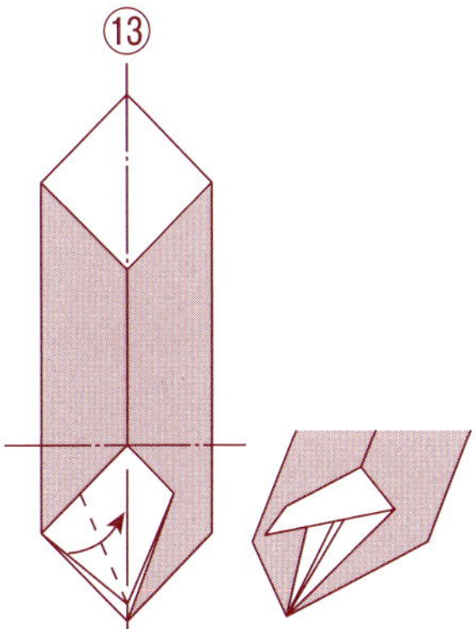

三角形を開きます
Open up the triangle

角ⓐを右下角に合わせて折り**右側に三角形**を作ります
Fold the corner ⓐ to the right lower corner to make a triangle on the right side

⑬ ⑭ ⑮

折りすじに合わせて**内側に折ります**
Fold inwards along the lines

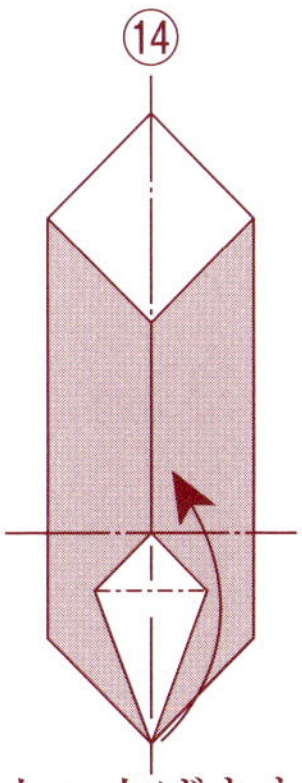

上へ上げます
Fold up

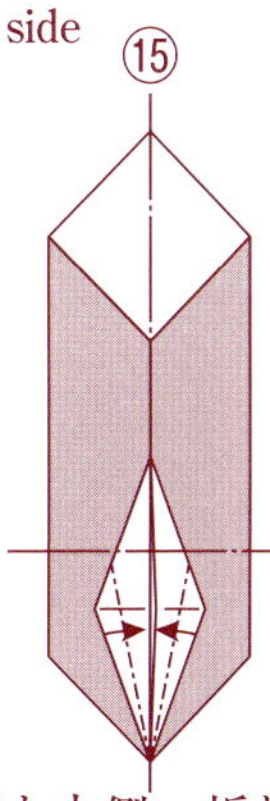

両側を内側へ折ります
Fold the both sides inwards

37

③

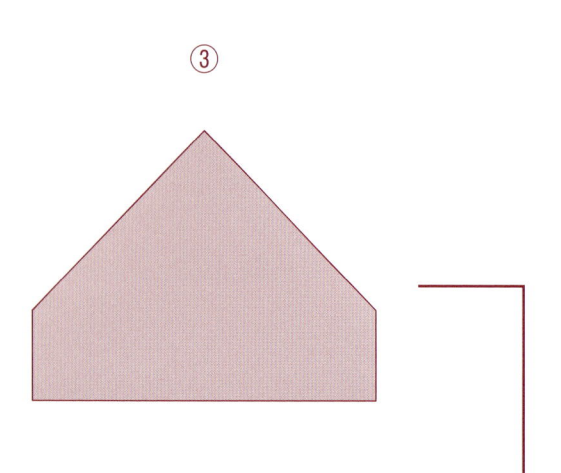

④

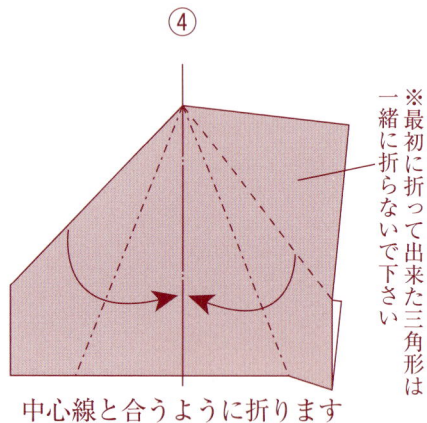

中心線と合うように折ります
Fold to the center line
※ Leave the triangles unfolded

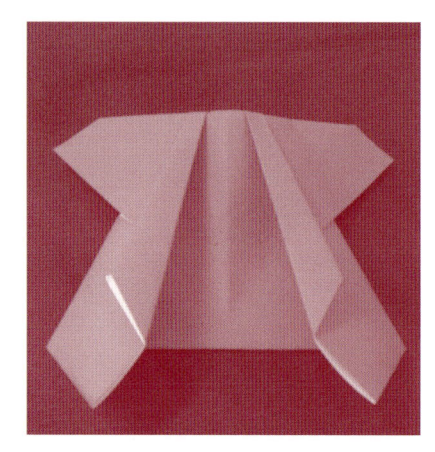

※最初に折って出来た三角形は一緒に折らないで下さい

平成になり還暦を迎えても、若く、60歳を自分流の出発の歳とされる方々も多く、昭和以前の年祝いと異なり"赤いちゃんちゃんこ"を着てお祝いをする風習も遠くなりました。特に、両親など、親しい方々への還暦祝いには、改まらず、日本の古き良き伝統を残し、赤いちゃんちゃんこ形の祝い袋を作りましょう。

Nowadays sixty-year-old people are young at heart and ready to enjoy their second lives. It would be appropriate to give money packaged in the form of "Chancanko".

・紙＝赤い紙（片面でも、両面でも赤が必要）
　　寸法　お金を入れる封筒のタテの２倍の
　　　　　正方形
・金封＝無地白封筒又は半紙

上書きには「還暦御祝いおめでとう、いつまでも若く」などのメッセージを添えて…

Paper : red paper (red on one side or both sides)
Size : square paper twice as large as the longer size of a money envelope
Money envelope : a white envelope or Hanshi (writing paper)

Messages such as "Congratulation on your Kanreki, Stay young" on the front

⑨

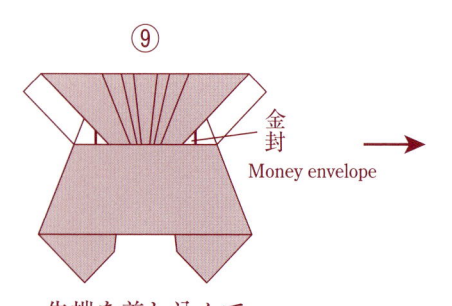

金封
Money envelope

先端を差し込んで
金封を覆います
Insert the tip to cover
the money envelope

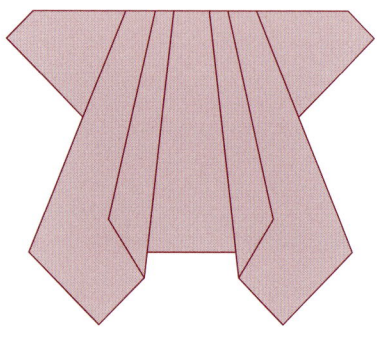

表へ向けて完成です
Turn to the front
Completed

38

親しい方への還暦祝い Kanreki celebration

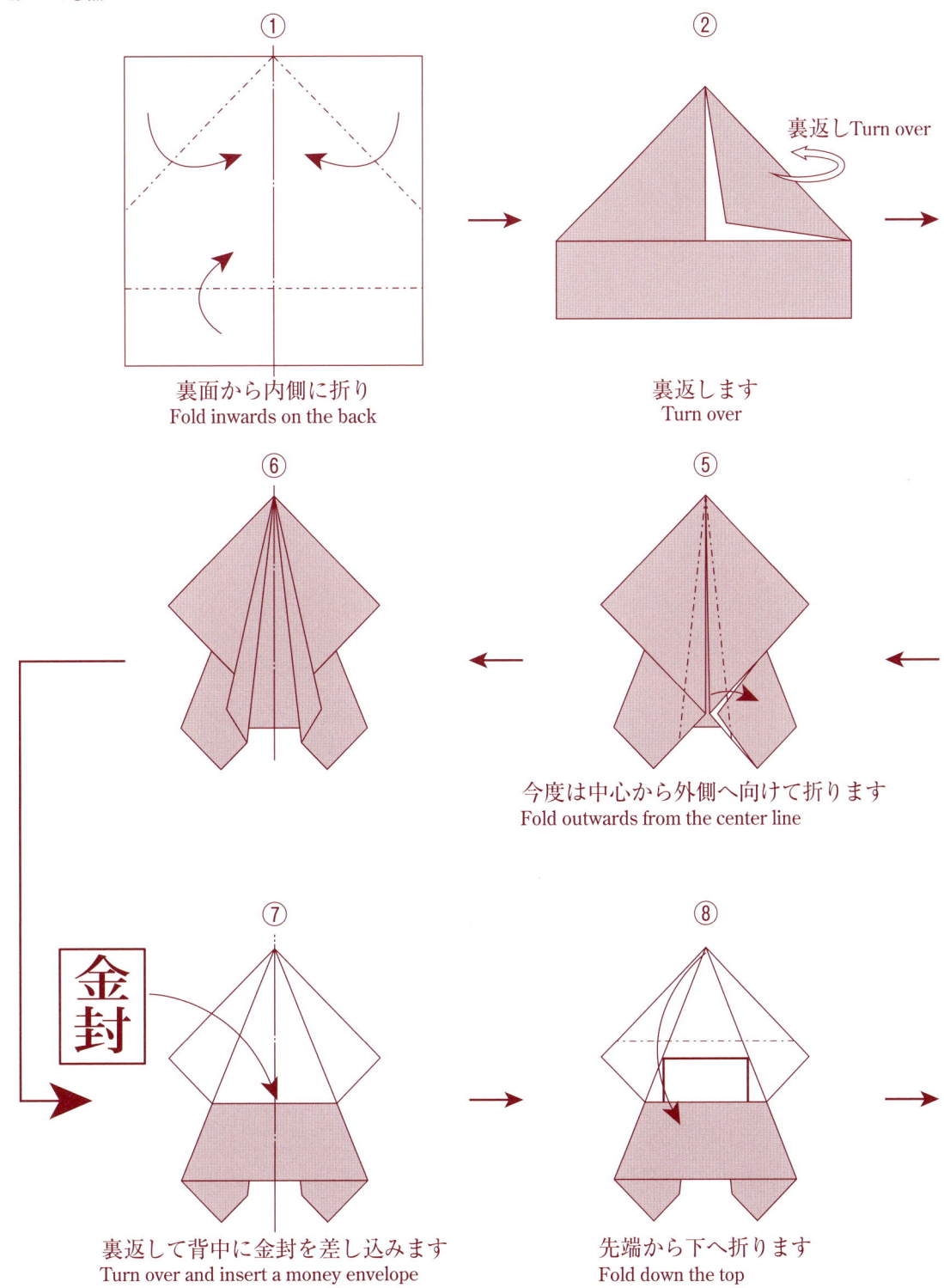

18-19ページ参照

① 裏面から内側に折り
Fold inwards on the back

② 裏返します
Turn over / 裏返し Turn over

⑤ 今度は中心から外側へ向けて折ります
Fold outwards from the center line

⑥

⑦ 金封
裏返して背中に金封を差し込みます
Turn over and insert a money envelope

⑧ 先端から下へ折ります
Fold down the top

39

④

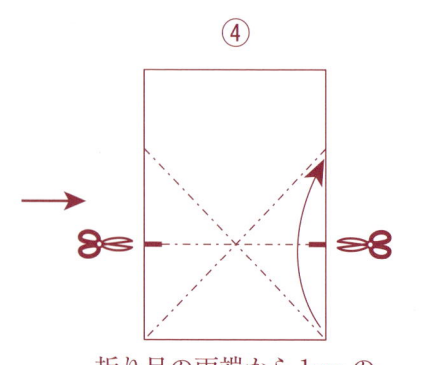

折り目の両端から1cmの
切り込みを入れ、折り合わせます
Cut by 1cm on the both sides and fold up

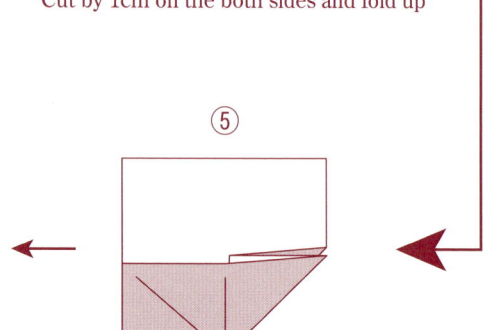

⑤

両側を折り目に合わせ
中折りにします
Inside reverse fold along the lines

⑫

水引をVの字に折ります
Bend Mizuhiki (a paper string)
into the V shape

⑬

両面テープ等で千代紙を
兜に貼って水引をとめます
Stick Mizuhiki on Kabuto by Chiyogami
(paper with colored figures) with a
double-sided tape

男の子の初節句の御祝い金封
Money envelope on the first festival for a boy

紙＝長方形の色和紙
寸法：お札のタテの長さに合わせ、紙を選んで下さい。

Paper : rectangular colored paper
Size : Choose paper according to the size of bills

例：1万円札の場合 A3の紙を用意。
Example : Prepare A-3 sized paper for 10,000 yen bills

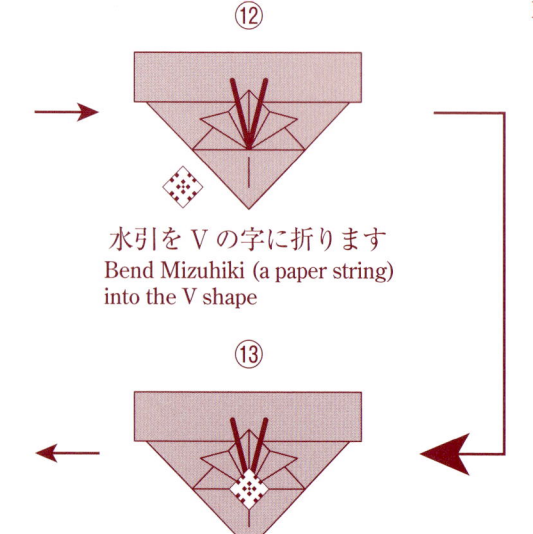

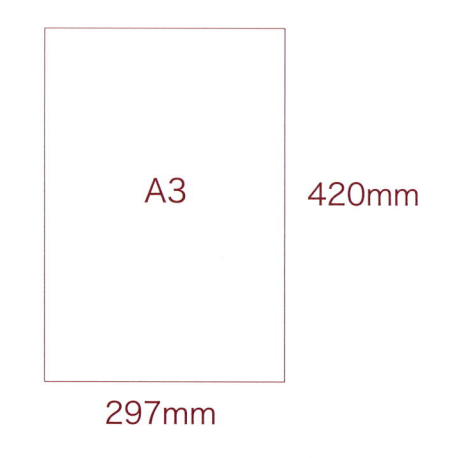

A3 420mm
297mm

40

兜のポチ袋 Kabuto (Samurai worrier helmet) petit envelope

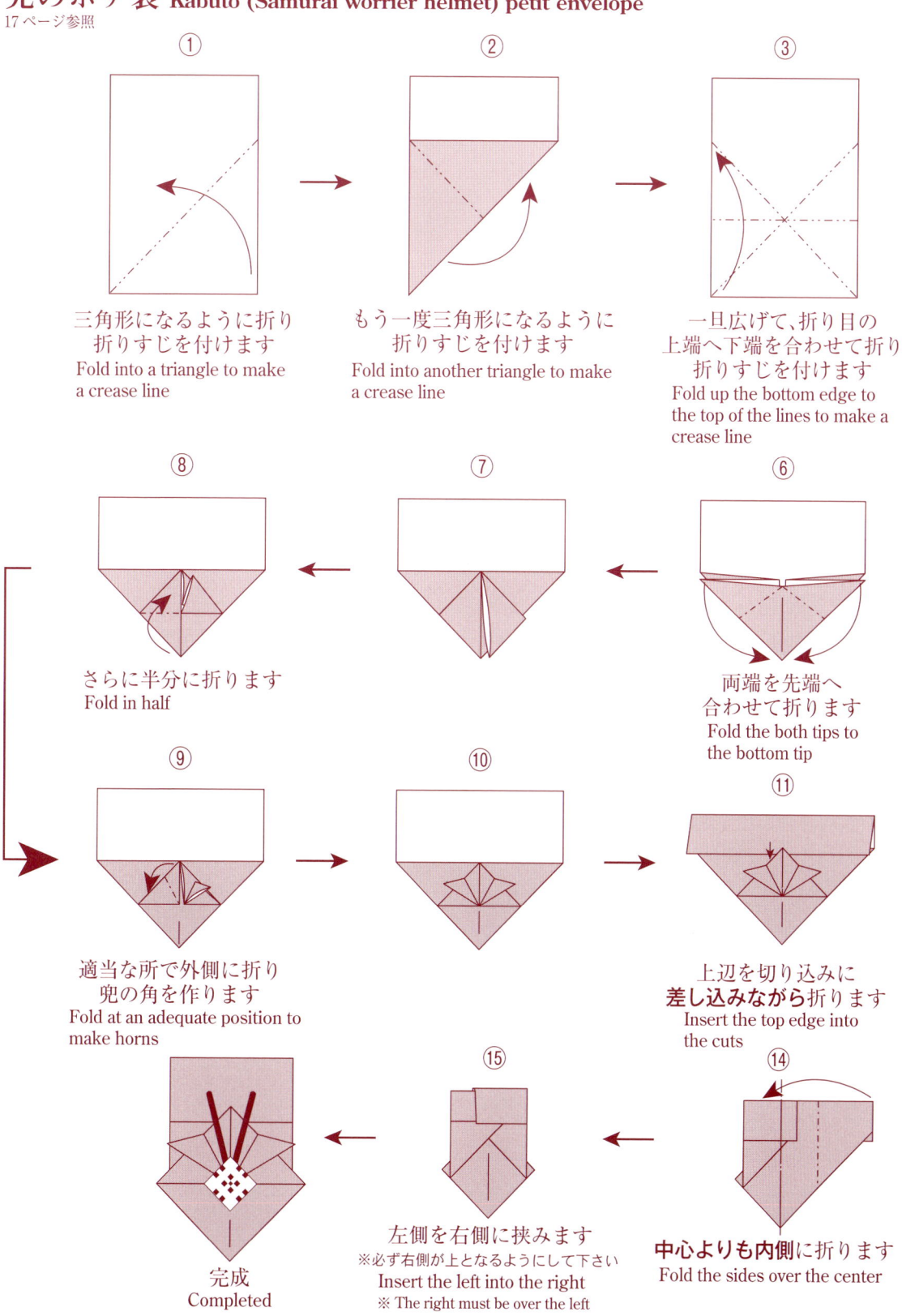

17ページ参照

① 三角形になるように折り折りすじを付けます
Fold into a triangle to make a crease line

② もう一度三角形になるように折りすじを付けます
Fold into another triangle to make a crease line

③ 一旦広げて、折り目の上端へ下端を合わせて折り折りすじを付けます
Fold up the bottom edge to the top of the lines to make a crease line

⑥ 両端を先端へ合わせて折ります
Fold the both tips to the bottom tip

⑦

⑧ さらに半分に折ります
Fold in half

⑨ 適当な所で外側に折り兜の角を作ります
Fold at an adequate position to make horns

⑩

⑪ 上辺を切り込みに差し込みながら折ります
Insert the top edge into the cuts

⑭ 中心よりも内側に折ります
Fold the sides over the center

⑮ 左側を右側に挟みます
※必ず右側が上となるようにして下さい
Insert the left into the right
※ The right must be over the left

完成
Completed

41

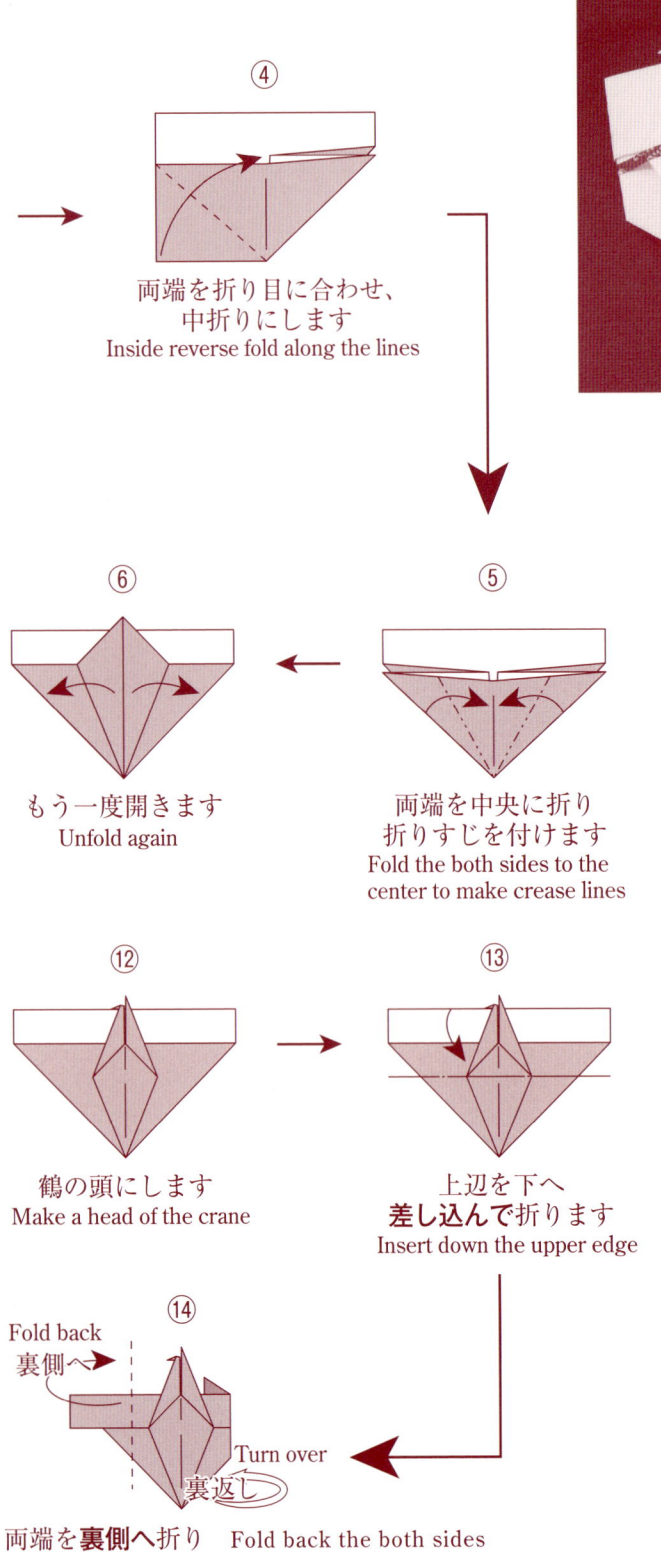

④
両端を折り目に合わせ、
中折りにします
Inside reverse fold along the lines

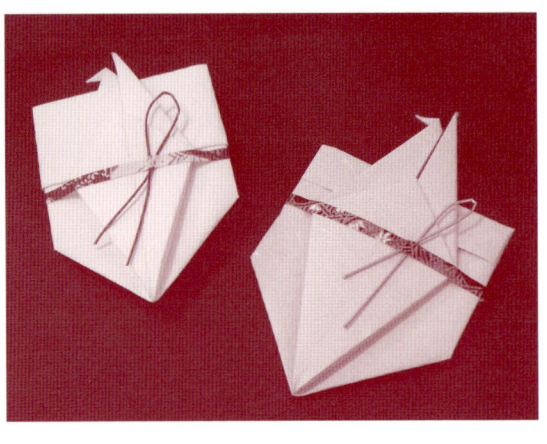

・お金（お札、コイン）

・香り

・針供養（針、糸を入れる）

※古くは琴爪、へその緒なども
　入れたと言われています。

・Money (bills and coins)

・Incense

・Hari-kuyo (worship for broken needles and strings wishing improvement of sawing)

※Koto (a Japanese zither) plectrums and an umbilical cord in the past

⑥
もう一度開きます
Unfold again

⑤
両端を中央に折り
折りすじを付けます
Fold the both sides to the center to make crease lines

⑫
鶴の頭にします
Make a head of the crane

⑬
上辺を下へ
差し込んで折ります
Insert down the upper edge

⑭
Fold back
裏側へ
Turn over
裏返し

両端を**裏側へ**折り　Fold back the both sides
裏返します　　　　　and turn over

42

鶴ポチ袋 Crane petit envelope
21 ページ参照

① 三角形になるように折り折りすじを付けます
Fold into a triangle to make a crease line

② もう一度三角形になるように折りすじを付けます
Fold into another triangle to make a crease line

③ 一旦広げて、折り目の上端へ下端を合わせて折り折りすじを付けます
Fold up the bottom edge to the top of the lines to make a crease line

⑨ 中心線に合わせて裏側へ折り4箇所に折りすじを付けます
Fold back along the center line to make four crease lines

⑧ 反対側へ開きます
Open to the opposite side

⑦ 折り目に沿って中折りにします
Inside reverse fold along the lines

⑩ 4箇所全てに折りすじを付けた際出来たⓐを基準に図の様に中折りにします
Inside reverse fold at ⓐ of the lines

この部分が尖るように折って下さい
Fold to peak the corner

⑪ 左側を中折りにします
Inside reverse fold the left part

⑮ 右側を上にして左側を差し込みます
Insert the left side into the right side

完成
Completed

43

④

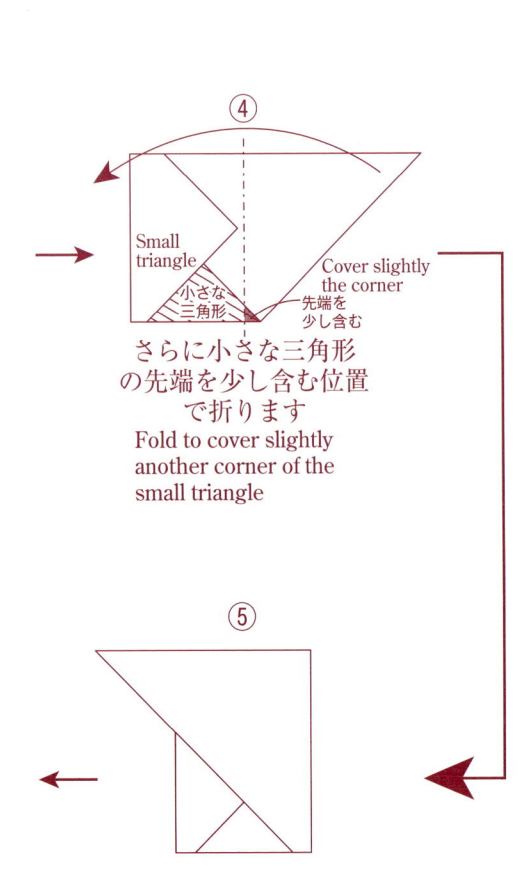

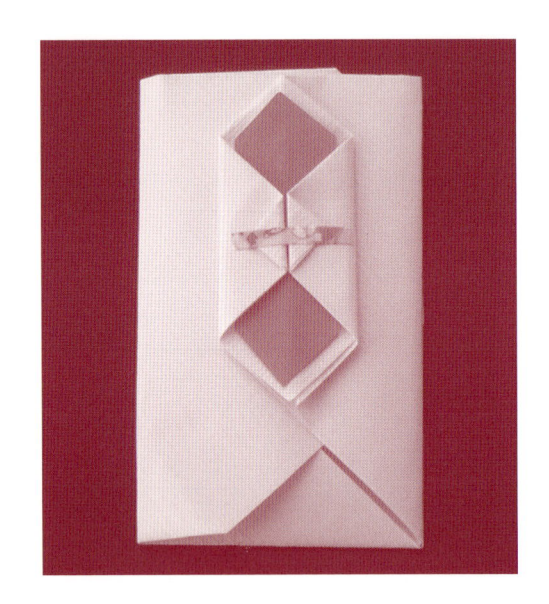

Small triangle
小さな三角形

Cover slightly the corner
先端を少し含む

さらに小さな三角形
の先端を少し含む位置
で折ります
Fold to cover slightly another corner of the small triangle

⑤

・慶事のお金包み
・ご招待状入れ
・内祝いの小風呂敷
・ハンカチ
・葉書 etc

・Celebratory money
・Invitation
・Wrapping cloth on Uchiiwai (private celebration gifts)
・Handkerchief
・Post card

44

葉書包み Post card envelope

5ページ参照

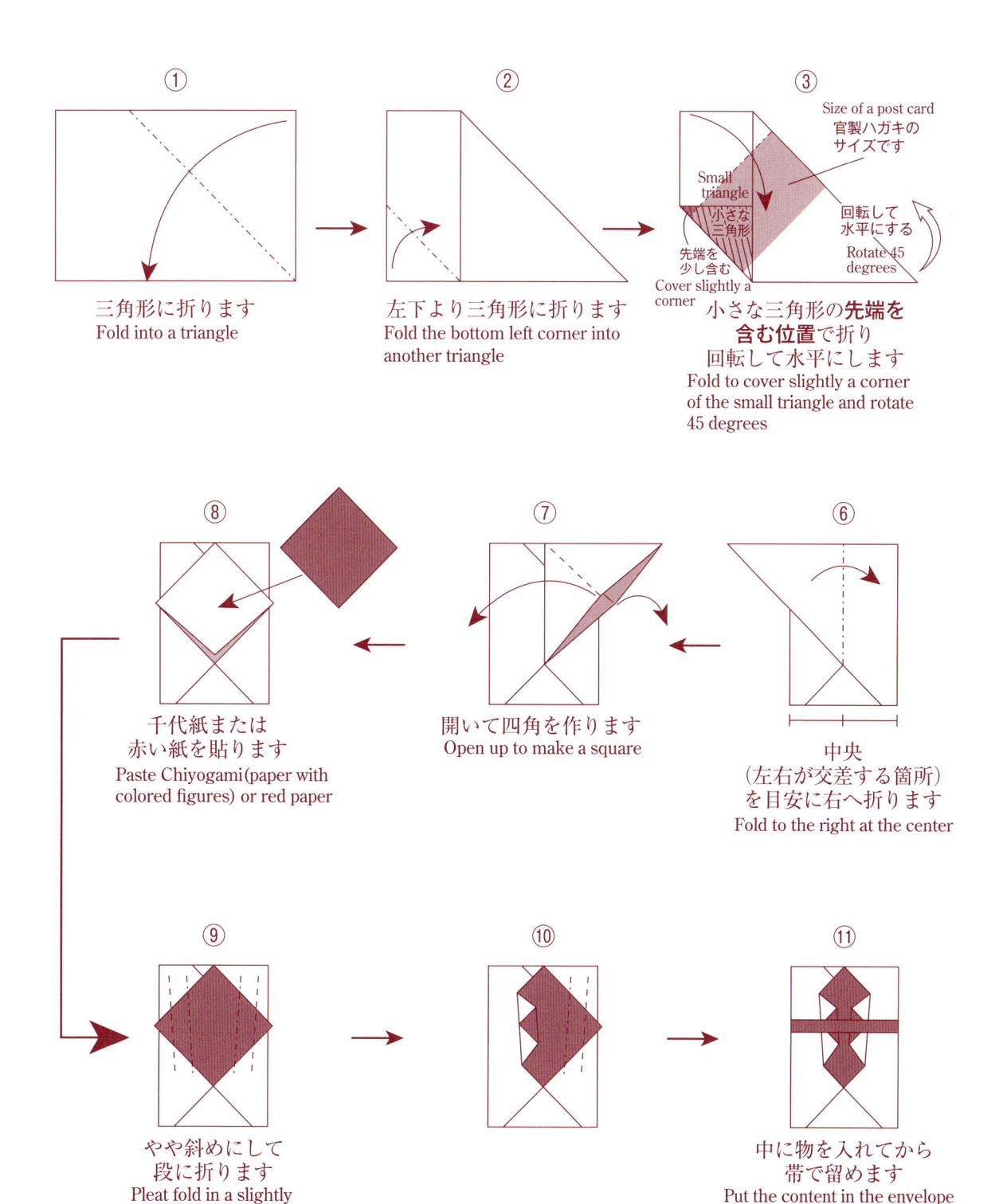

① 三角形に折ります
Fold into a triangle

② 左下より三角形に折ります
Fold the bottom left corner into another triangle

③ Size of a post card 官製ハガキのサイズです
Small triangle 小さな三角形
先端を少し含む Cover slightly a corner
回転して水平にする Rotate 45 degrees
小さな三角形の**先端を含む位置**で折り回転して水平にします
Fold to cover slightly a corner of the small triangle and rotate 45 degrees

⑥ 中央（左右が交差する箇所）を目安に右へ折ります
Fold to the right at the center

⑦ 開いて四角を作ります
Open up to make a square

⑧ 千代紙または赤い紙を貼ります
Paste Chiyogami(paper with colored figures) or red paper

⑨ やや斜めにして段に折ります
Pleat fold in a slightly tilted manner

⑩

⑪ 中に物を入れてから帯で留めます
Put the content in the envelope and tie it with Obi(band)

45

④

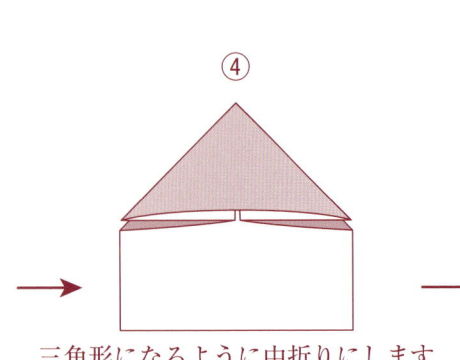

三角形になるように中折りにします
Inside reverse fold along the lines

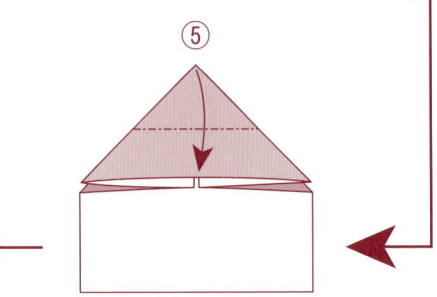

⑤

頂点を三角形の底辺に
合わせて折ります
Fold the top to the bottom
edge of the triangle

神仏へお供えをする際に用いられ、白い紙(書道用の半紙)を使用し、収穫を感謝して、米・豆等の五穀を入れました。
As offerings to the Shinto's gods and Buddha, a package in Hanshi (writing paper) contains five grains such as rice and beans giving thanks for prosperity and good harvest.

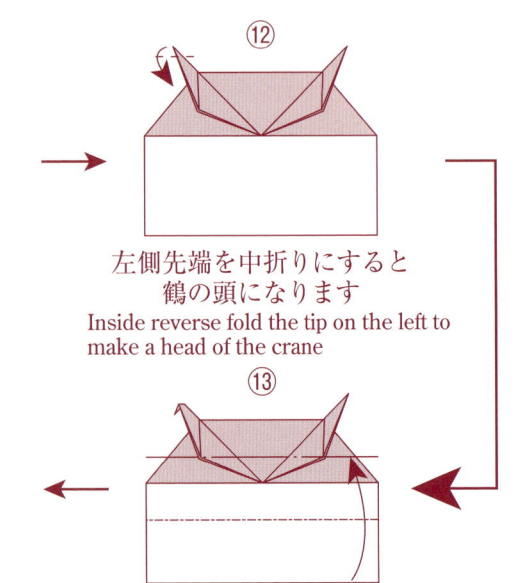

⑫

左側先端を中折りにすると
鶴の頭になります
Inside reverse fold the tip on the left to
make a head of the crane

⑬

頭と尾羽の角に合わせて
下端を折り上げます
Fold up the bottom edge to the
bases of the neck and the tail

46

供え物包み Offering package

5ページ参照

① 三角形になるように折り折りすじをつけます
Fold into a triangle to make a crease line

② もう一度三角形になるように折りすじをつけます
Fold into another triangle to make a crease line

③ 折りすじをつけたら一度拡げ、折り目に沿って
Unfold

⑥ 両側に三角形ができます
Two triangles on the sides

⑦ 両側の三角形の中心を上辺に合わせて折ります
Fold up the centers of the triangles to the upper edge

⑧ 四角形を作りさらに対角線に合わせて折りすじをつけます
Fold into a square to make crease lines along the diagonal lines

⑨ 折りすじに合わせて内側へ折ります
Fold inwards along the lines

⑩ それぞれを上に折り上げます
Fold up the each part

⑪ 下へ折りたたみます
Fold down

⑭ 折り上げた上端から1/3程度の所へもう一度折り上げます
Fold up the bottom edge to one third below the folded edge

⑮ 首と尾羽の付け根で両端を裏側へ折ります
Fold back 裏へ Fold back 裏へ
Fold back the both sides at the bases of the neck and the tail

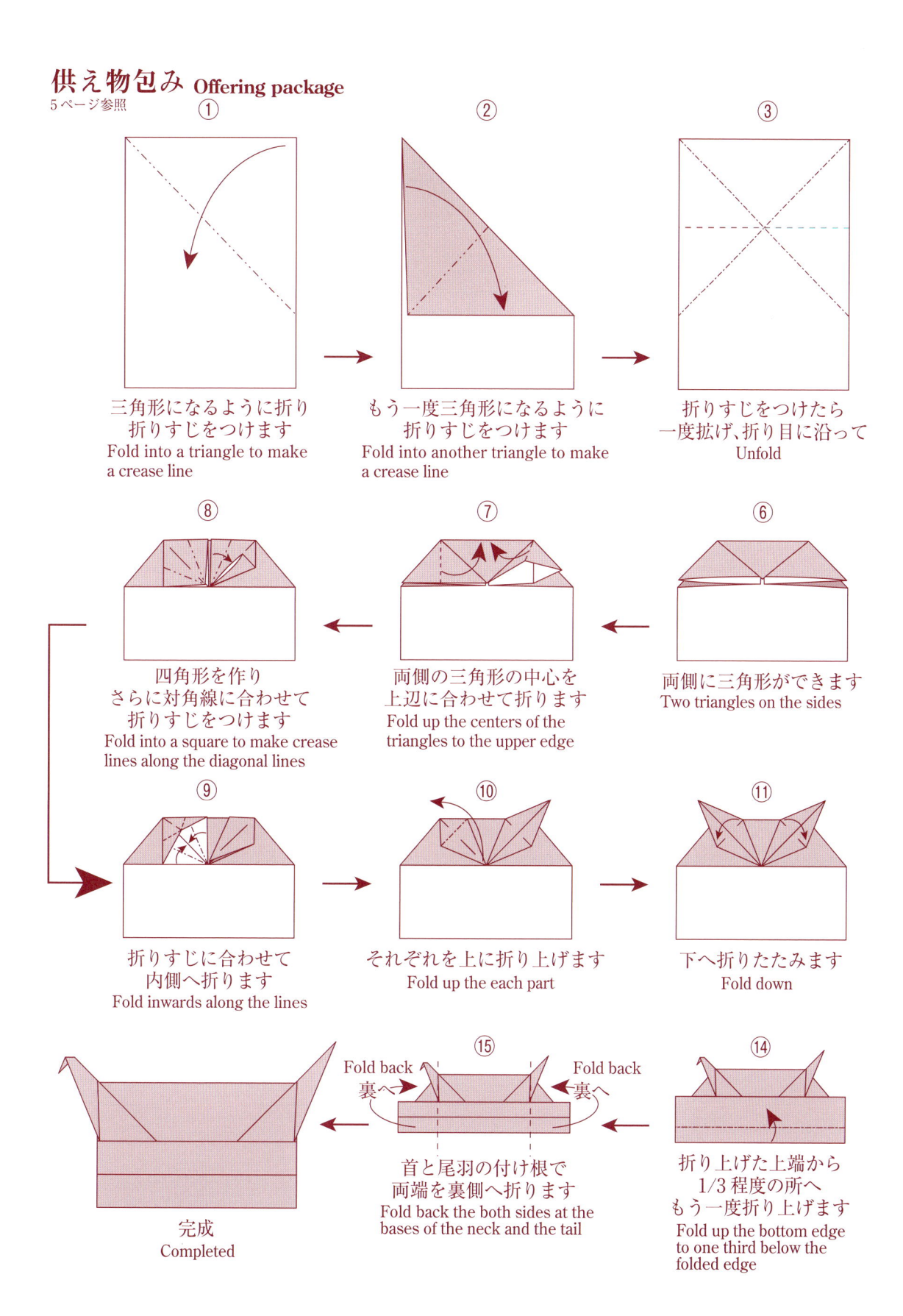

完成
Completed

47

④

右1/3の箇所に
折りすじを付けます
Make a crease line one third
from the right edge

⑤

右下角を左上に折り
折りすじを付けます
Fold up the right bottom tip
towards the upper left

⑫

下端を上へ折ります
Fold up the bottom edge

48

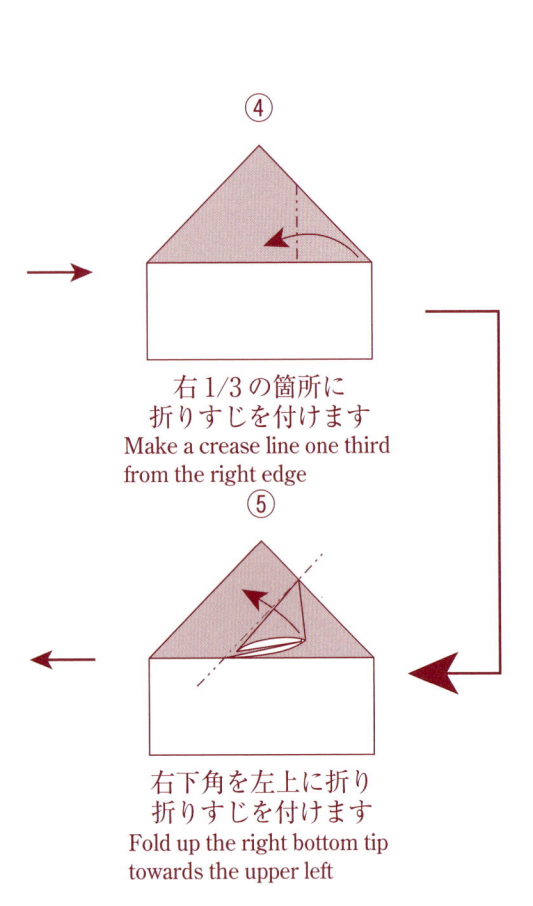

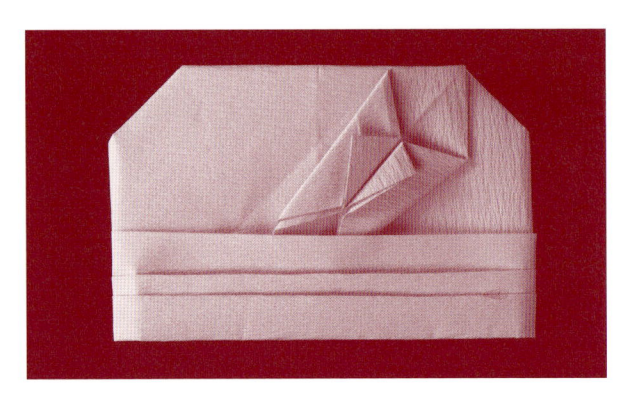

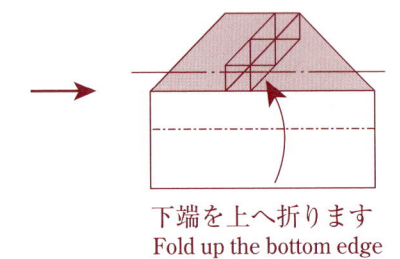

略式紙幣包み Informal money envelope

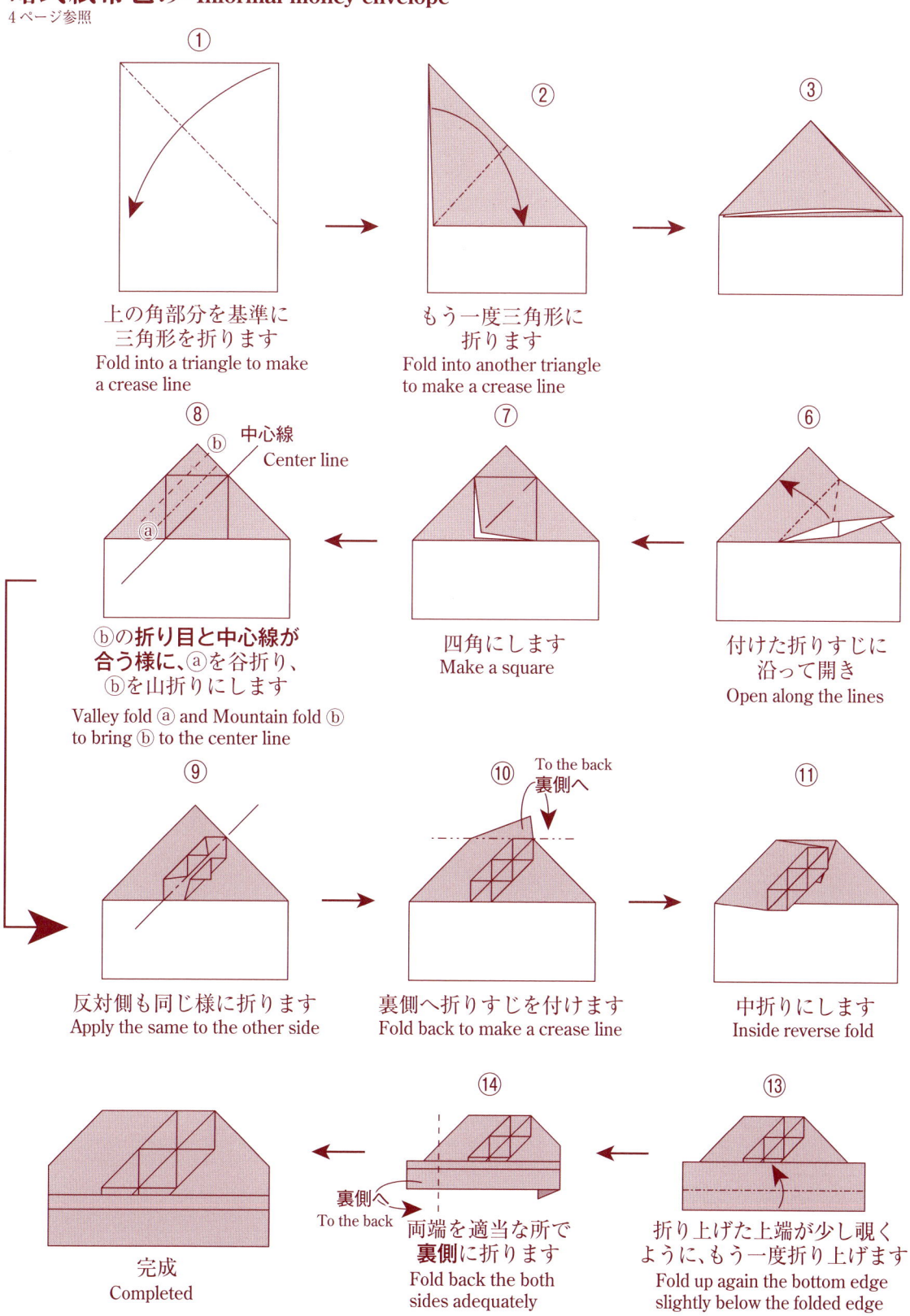

4ページ参照

① 上の角部分を基準に三角形を折ります
Fold into a triangle to make a crease line

② もう一度三角形に折ります
Fold into another triangle to make a crease line

③

⑥ 付けた折りすじに沿って開き
Open along the lines

⑦ 四角にします
Make a square

⑧ 中心線 Center line
ⓑの折り目と中心線が合う様に、ⓐを谷折り、ⓑを山折りにします
Valley fold ⓐ and Mountain fold ⓑ to bring ⓑ to the center line

⑨ 反対側も同じ様に折ります
Apply the same to the other side

⑩ 裏側へ To the back
裏側へ折りすじを付けます
Fold back to make a crease line

⑪ 中折りにします
Inside reverse fold

⑬ 折り上げた上端が少し覗くように、もう一度折り上げます
Fold up again the bottom edge slightly below the folded edge

⑭ 裏側へ To the back
両端を適当な所で裏側に折ります
Fold back the both sides adequately

完成
Completed

49

④ 両側を折ります
Fold up the both sides

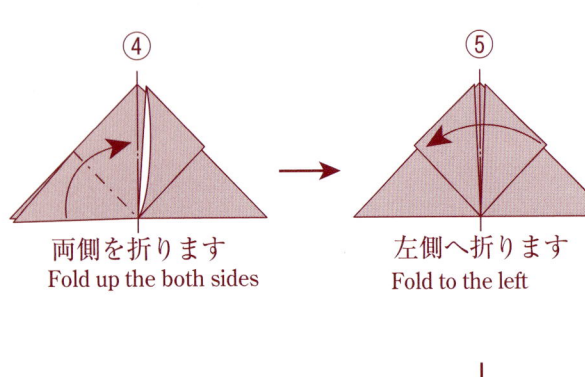

⑤ 左側へ折ります
Fold to the left

昭和のはじめの頃迄は、薬・胡麻・植物の種等を入れていた様です。
アクセサリー(指輪・イヤリング・ブローチ他)や小物を入れるプレゼントの包みにしてはいかがでしょう。
Up to the early-Showa era (around 1930's), it was used to contain medicine, sesame, or plant seeds. Suitable for gift packages of accessories such as rings, earrings and pins.

⑥ 谷、山、山と折ります
Valley, Mountain and Mountain fold

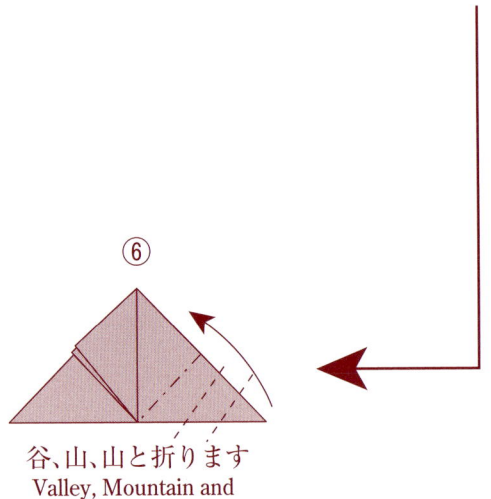

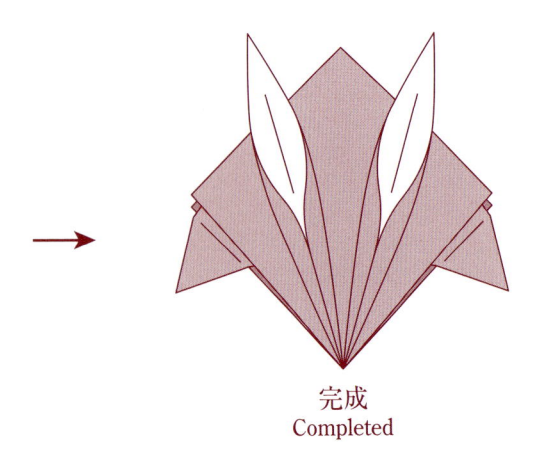

完成
Completed

50

うさぎたとう **Rabbit Tatou**
11ページ参照

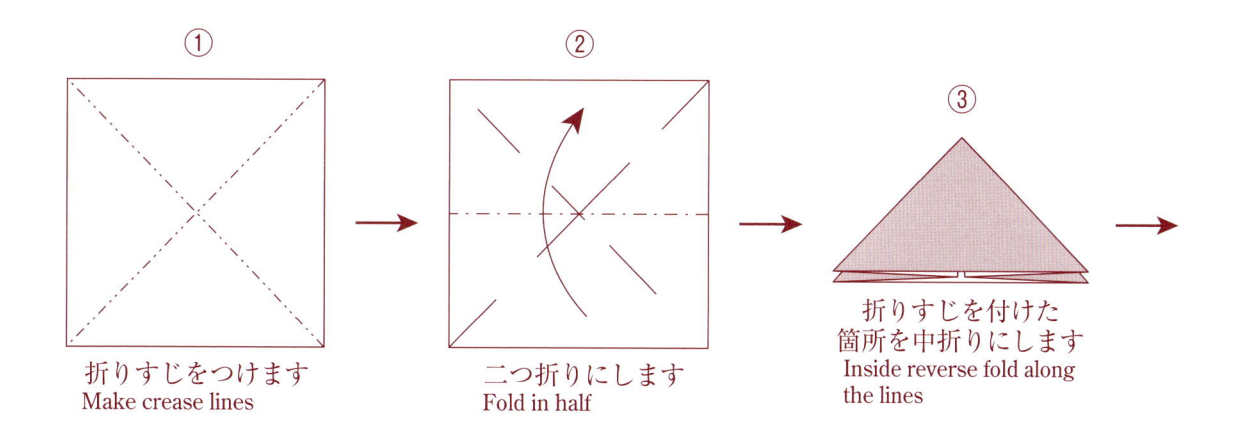

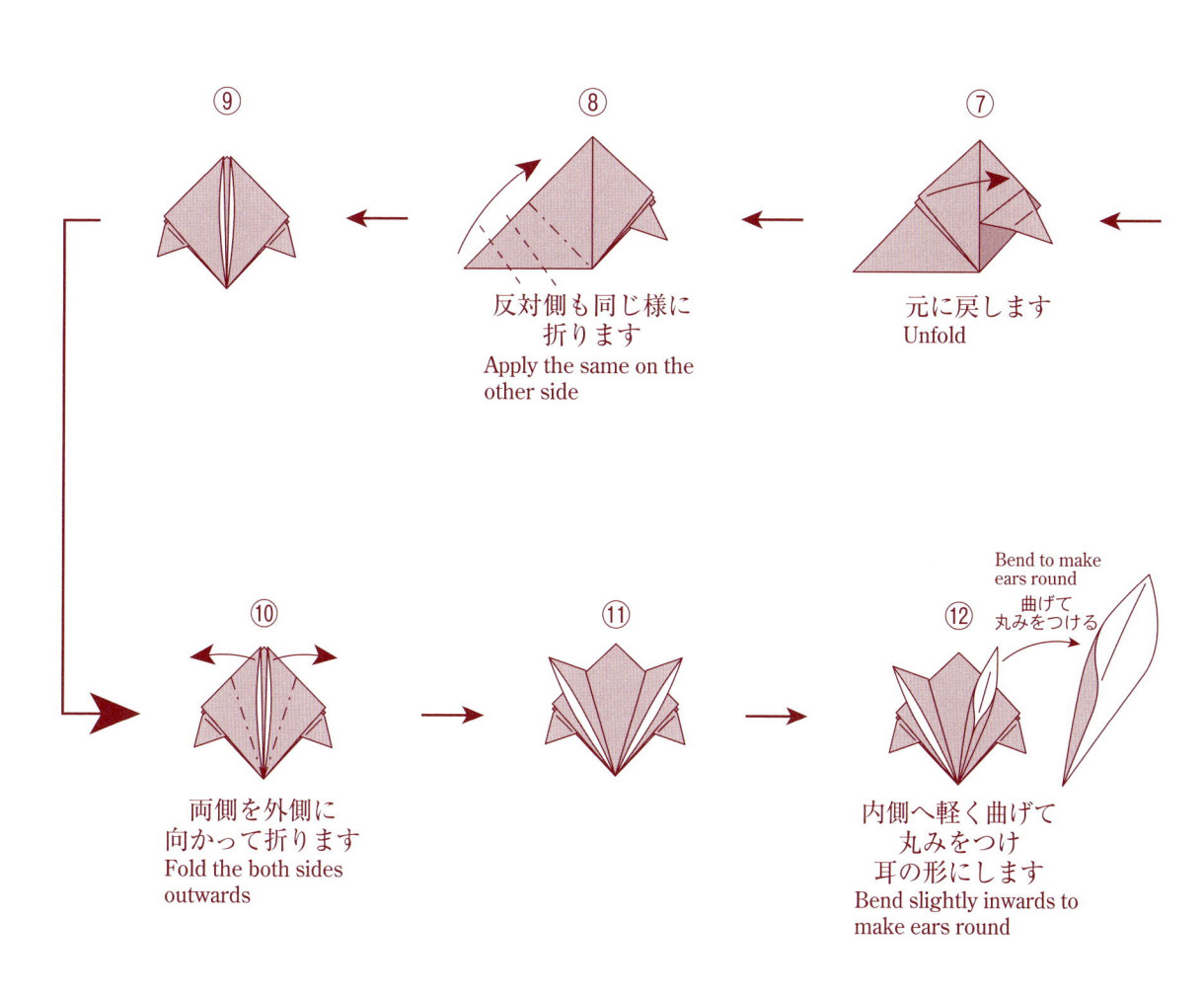

① 折りすじをつけます
Make crease lines

② 二つ折りにします
Fold in half

③ 折りすじを付けた箇所を中折りにします
Inside reverse fold along the lines

⑦ 元に戻します
Unfold

⑧ 反対側も同じ様に折ります
Apply the same on the other side

⑨

⑩ 両側を外側に向かって折ります
Fold the both sides outwards

⑪

⑫ 内側へ軽く曲げて丸みをつけ耳の形にします
Bend slightly inwards to make ears round

Bend to make ears round
曲げて丸みをつける

51

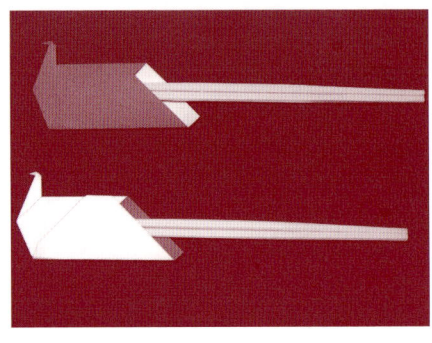

③ 三角形を開いて
四角形にします
Open the triangle
into a square

④

⑤ 対角線に合わせて
折りすじを付けます
Fold to the diagonal line
to make crease lines

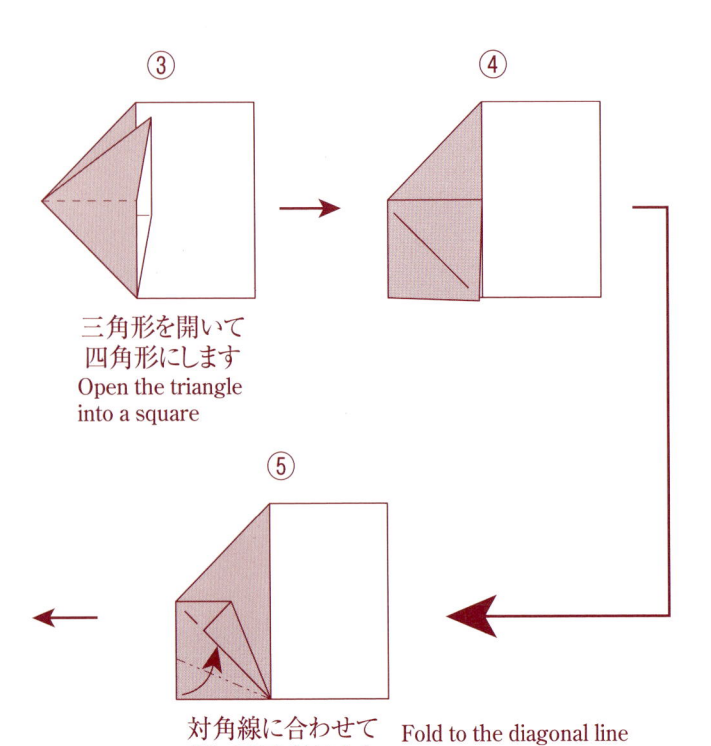

箸袋、黒文字入れ
紙のサイズを大きくする事で、
プレゼント用に、カードやチケットなどを入れる事が出来ます。
Chopstick case, Kuromoji case
In larger sizes, suitable for gift
envelopes for cards and tickets

⑩

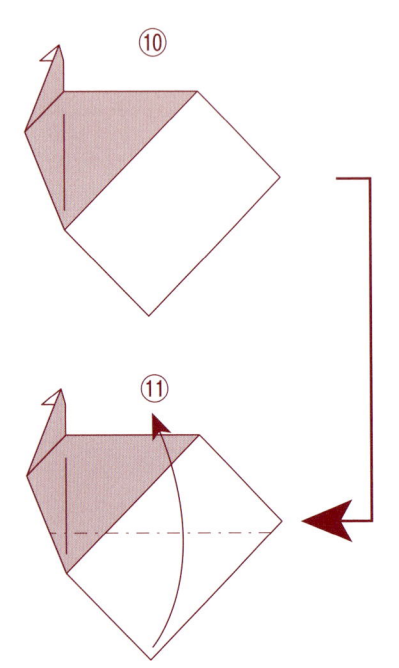

⑪ 先端が出る様に
上へ折ります
Fold up the tip over
the top edge

52

箸袋折鶴 Crane case

23ページ参照

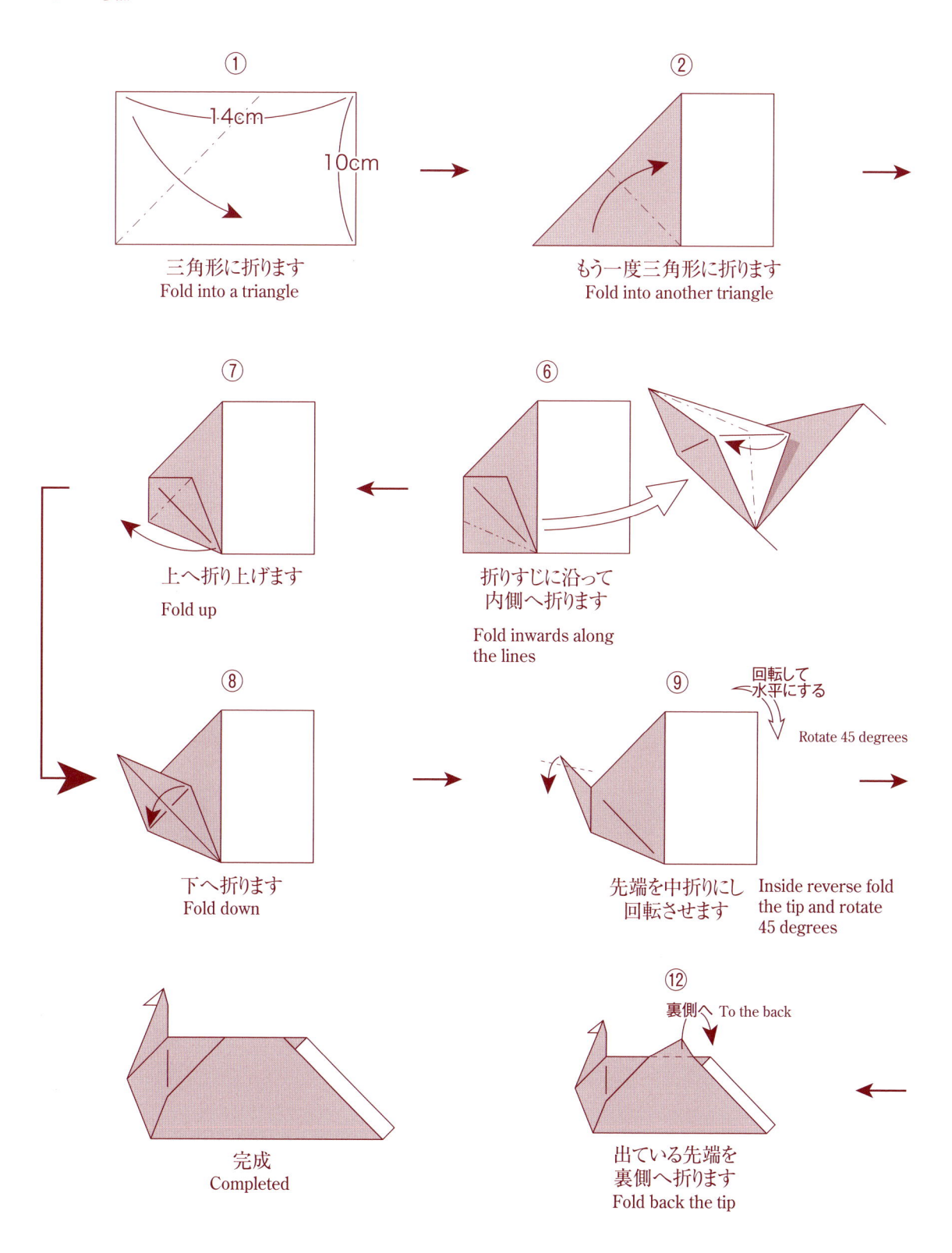

① 14cm / 10cm
三角形に折ります
Fold into a triangle

② もう一度三角形に折ります
Fold into another triangle

⑦ 上へ折り上げます
Fold up

⑥ 折りすじに沿って内側へ折ります
Fold inwards along the lines

⑧ 下へ折ります
Fold down

⑨ 先端を中折りにし回転させます
回転して水平にする
Rotate 45 degrees
Inside reverse fold the tip and rotate 45 degrees

完成
Completed

⑫ 出ている先端を裏側へ折ります
裏側へ To the back
Fold back the tip

53

③

新 札
New bills

新札を用意します
Prepare new bills

④

底に合わせて折ります
Fold the top tips to the
bottom edge

表完成図
Completed
(the front)

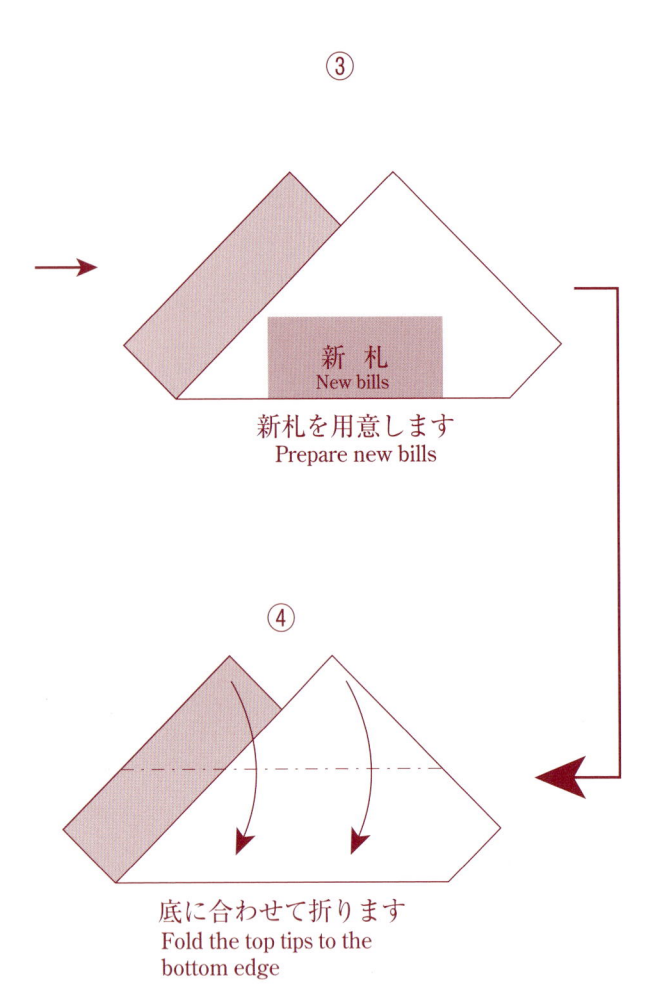

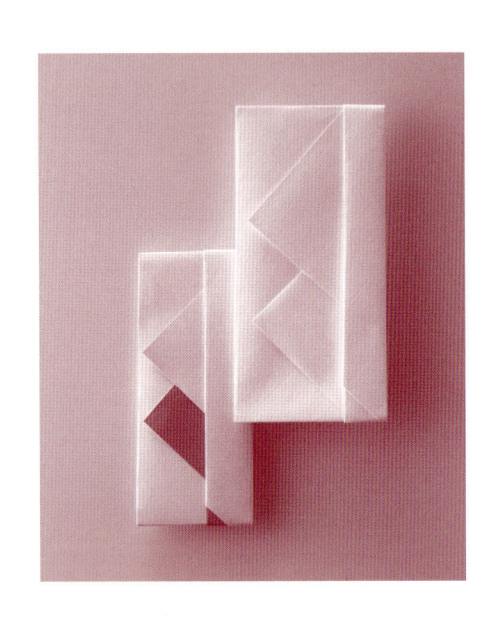

・お祝いは新札をそのまま入れます。

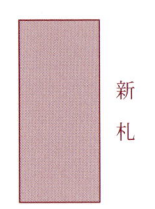

新札

Plane new bills for celebrations

・不幸事は新札を二つに折り、
　折り目をつけてから入れます。

新札に折り目をつける

New bills with a crease lines at
the center for condolences

基本のお金包み I Basic money envelope I
28ページ参照

①

② 水平にします
Rotate 45 degrees

Rotate 45 degrees

⑤ 新札 New bills
新札に合わせて下へ折り、回転します
Fold down to the size of the bills and rotate 90 degrees

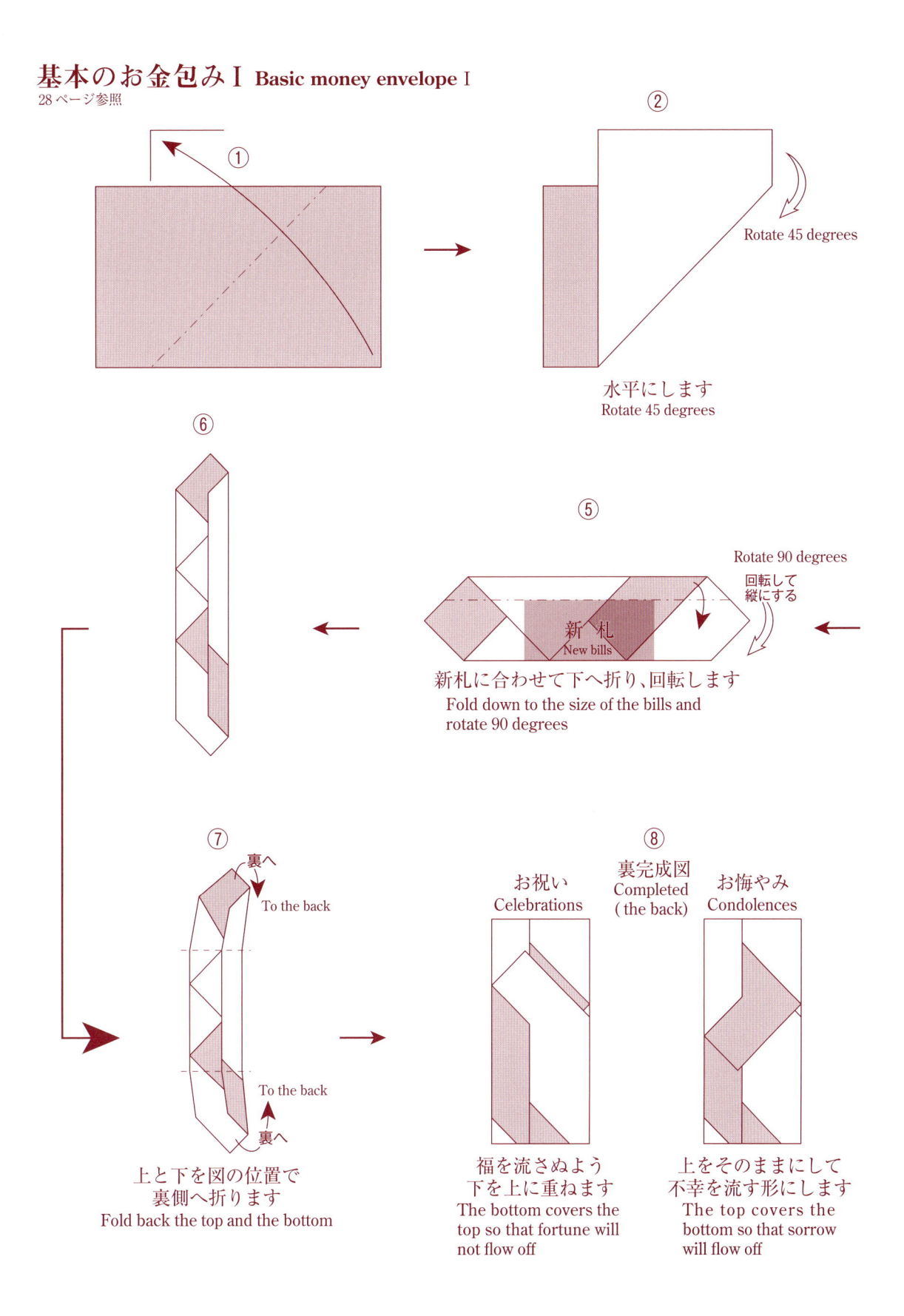

回転して縦にする
Rotate 90 degrees

⑥

⑦ 裏へ To the back
裏へ To the back
上と下を図の位置で裏側へ折ります
Fold back the top and the bottom

⑧ 裏完成図 Completed (the back)

お祝い Celebrations
福を流さぬよう下を上に重ねます
The bottom covers the top so that fortune will not flow off

お悔やみ Condolences
上をそのままにして不幸を流す形にします
The top covers the bottom so that sorrow will flow off

55

③

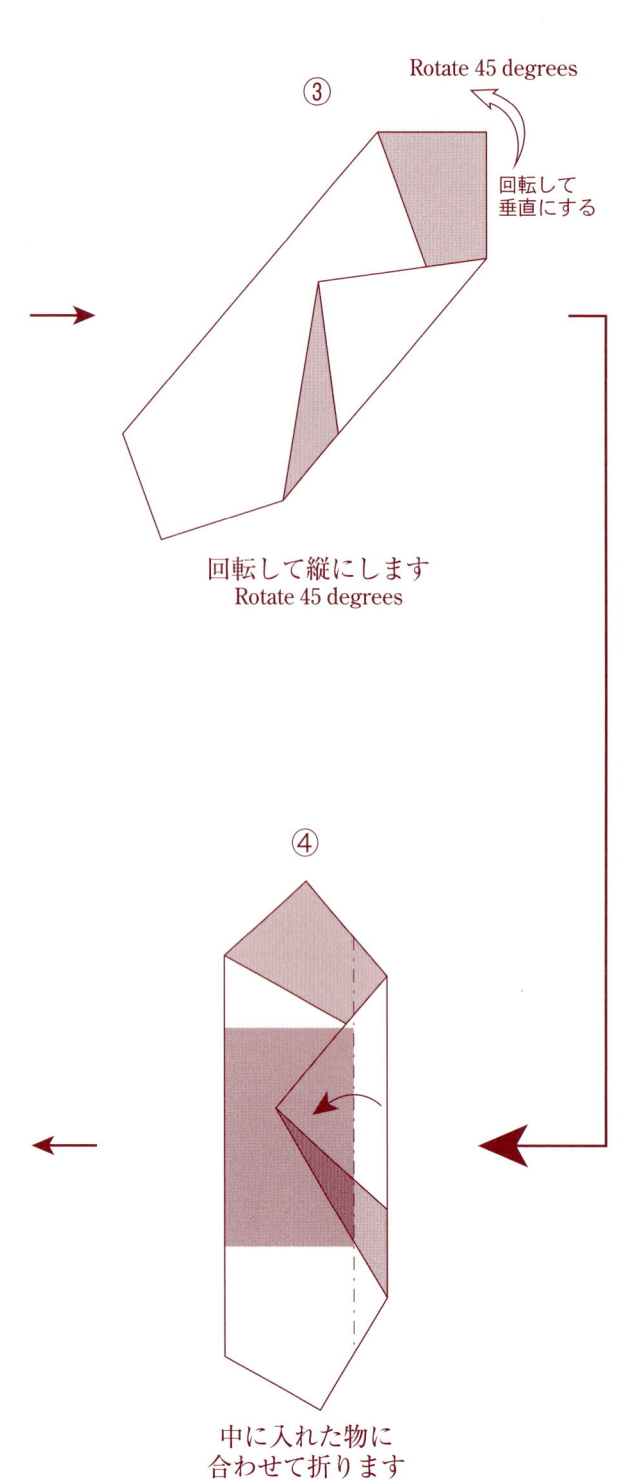

Rotate 45 degrees

回転して
垂直にする

回転して縦にします
Rotate 45 degrees

④

中に入れた物に
合わせて折ります
Fold to the size of the content

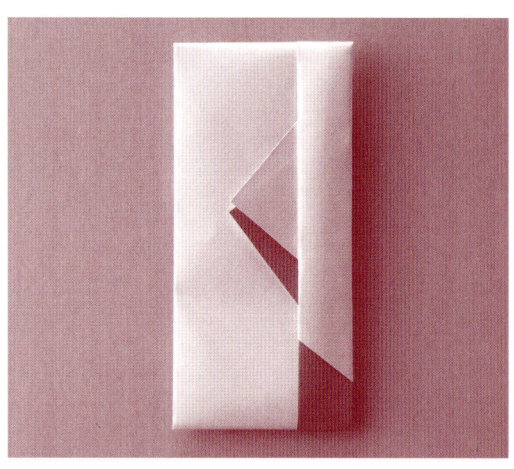

最も簡素な折かたです。小物を失わぬ様に、落とさぬ様に包む方法(かたち)です。
The simplest form of folding an envelope to keep small things safe

基本のお金包み II Basic money envelope II
28ページ参照

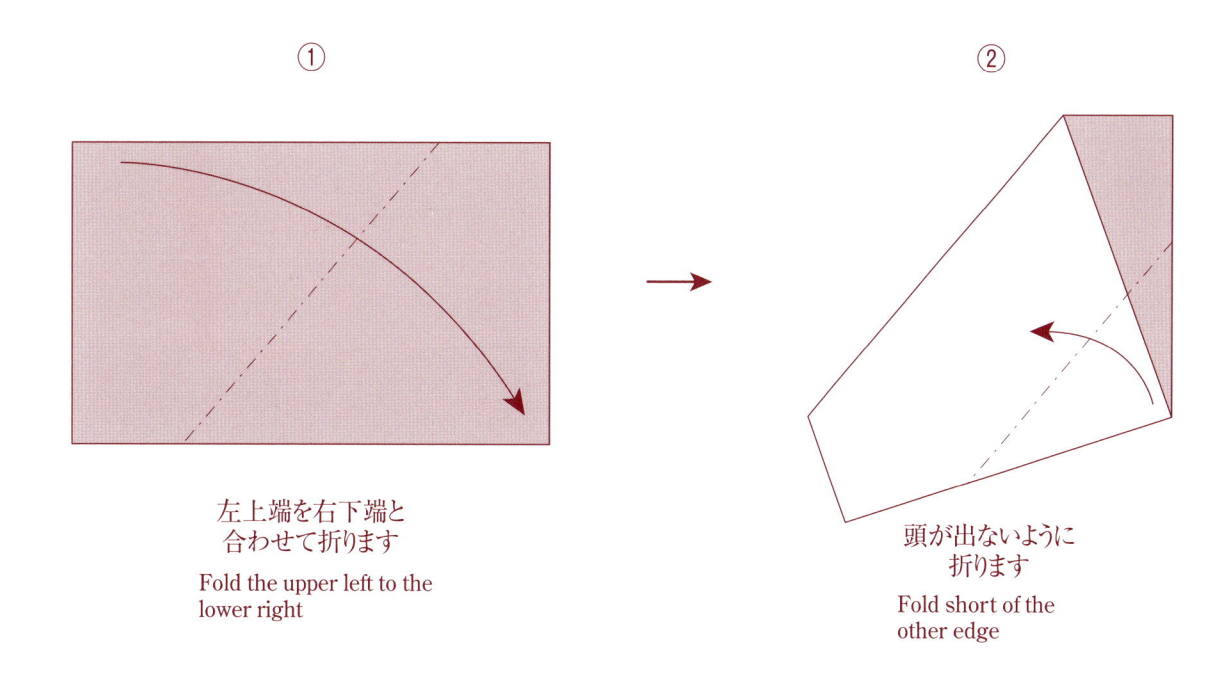

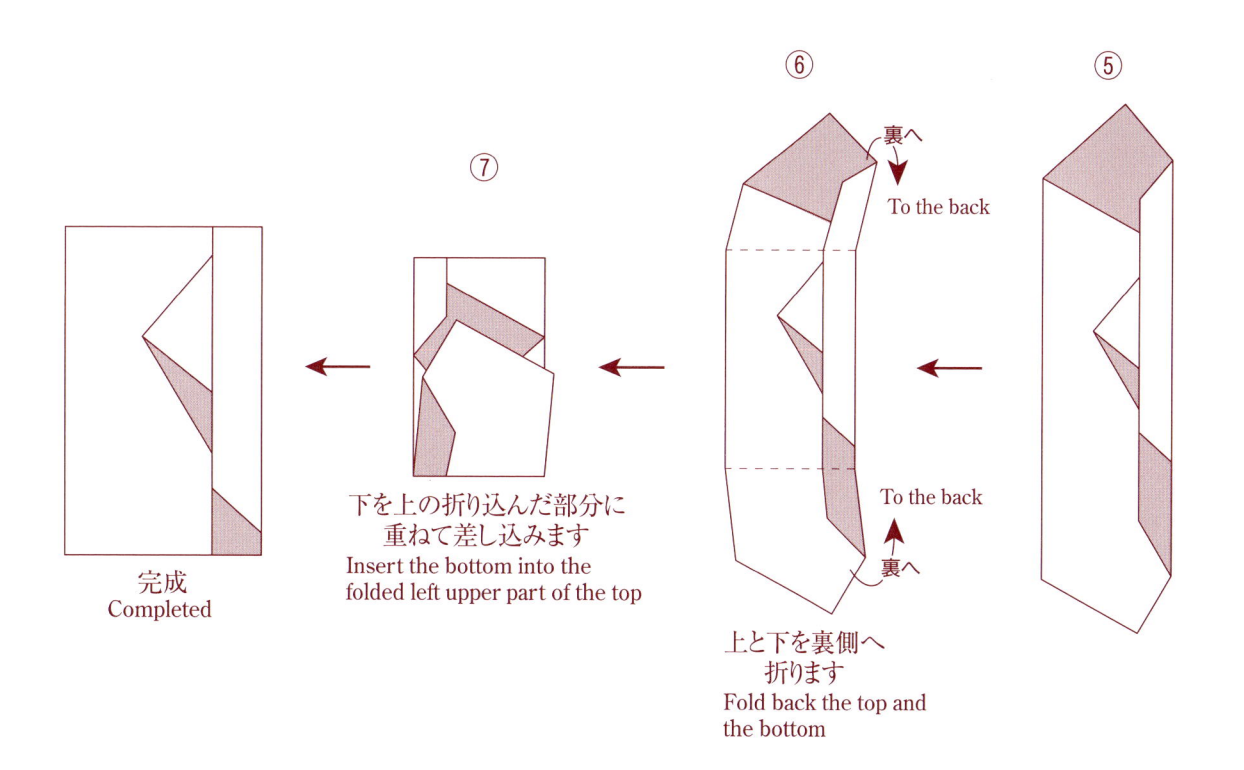

①

左上端を右下端と
合わせて折ります
Fold the upper left to the
lower right

②

頭が出ないように
折ります
Fold short of the
other edge

⑤

⑥ 裏へ
To the back

裏へ
To the back

上と下を裏側へ
折ります
Fold back the top and
the bottom

⑦

下を上の折り込んだ部分に
重ねて差し込みます
Insert the bottom into the
folded left upper part of the top

完成
Completed

④

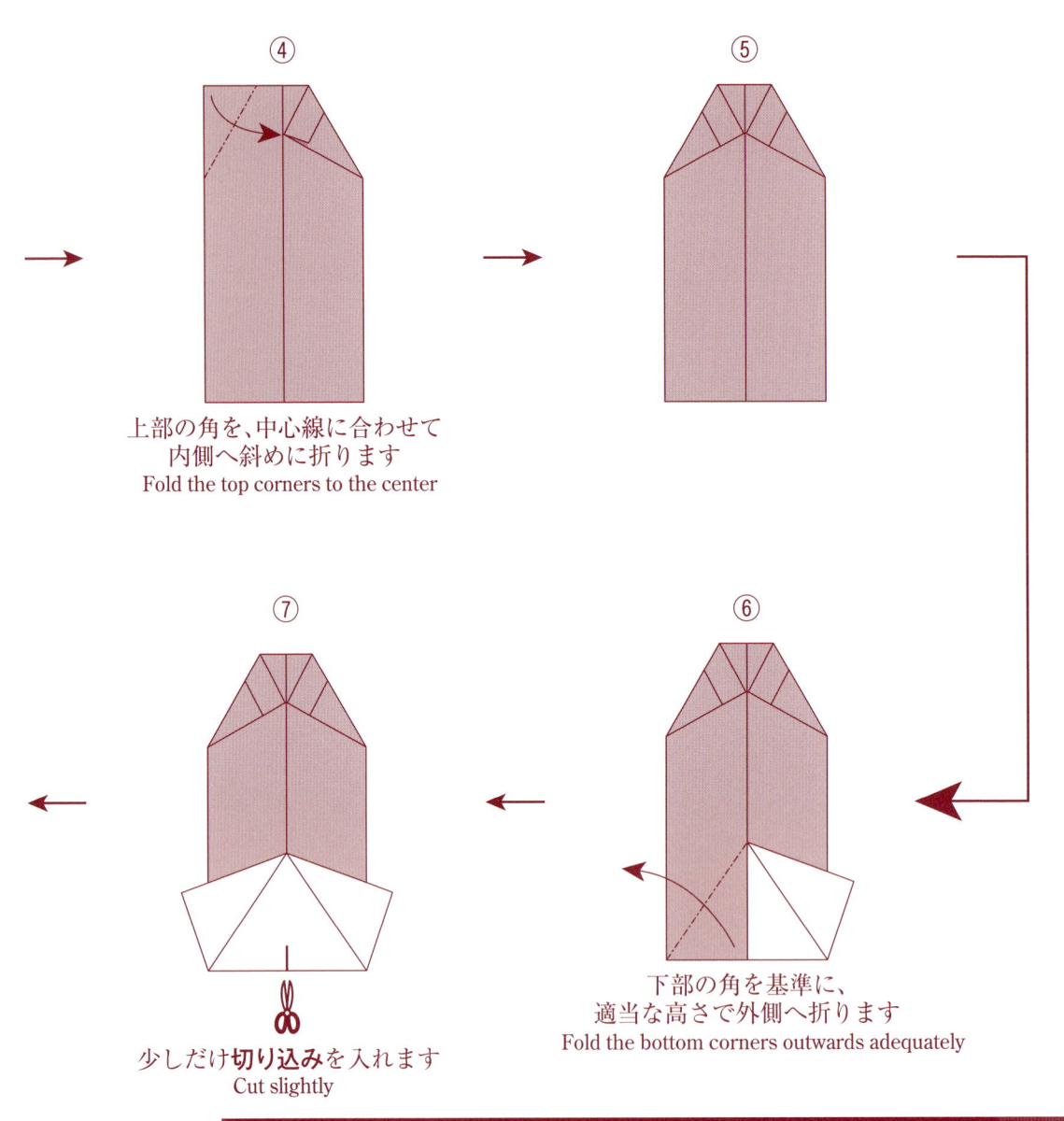

上部の角を、中心線に合わせて
内側へ斜めに折ります
Fold the top corners to the center

⑤

⑥

下部の角を基準に、
適当な高さで外側へ折ります
Fold the bottom corners outwards adequately

⑦

少しだけ**切り込み**を入れます
Cut slightly

シャツ　Shirt package

29ページ参照

① 包みたい物を中央よりやや上に置く

Place the content slightly above the center

②

③ 裏へ / To the back

上の適当な部分を**裏側へ**折ります
Fold back the top edge adequately

⑨

⑧

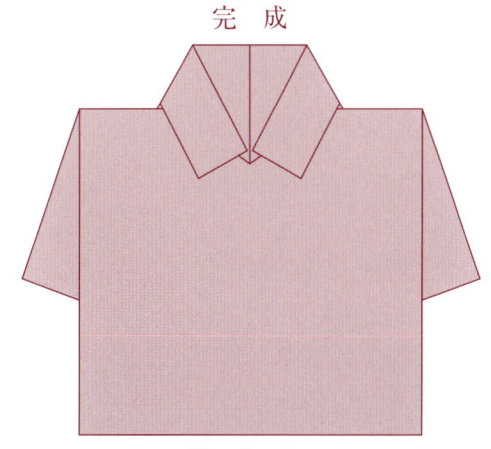

襟下に差し込んだら
下の部分を折ります
Put the bottom edge under the collars and fold the bottom edge

完　成

Completed

Index

Folding cranes for peace・・・・・・・・・・・・・・・2-3
   An authentic crane・・・・・・・・・・・・・・・・・34-35

Wrapping offerings to the gods・・・・・・・・・・4-5
   Post card envelope・・・・・・・・・・・・・・・・・44-45
   Offering package・・・・・・・・・・・・・・・・・・46-47
   Informal money envelope・・・・・・・・・・・・48-49

Japan wrapping culture・・・・・・・・・・・・・・・7-8
   Celebratory envelope・・・・・・・・・・・・・・・36-37

At the wedding ceremony・・・・・・・・・・・・・・9

Package of sesame・・・・・・・・・・・・・・・・・・10

Package of little items・・・・・・・・・・・・・・・・11
   Rabbit Tatou・・・・・・・・・・・・・・・・・・・・50-51

The five seasonal festivals・・・・・・・・・・・・・12

Hina festival・・・・・・・・・・・・・・・・・・・・・13

Tango-no-sekku・・・・・・・・・・・・・・・・・・・17
   Kabuto(Samurai worrier helmet) petit envelope
   ・・・・・・・・・・・・・・・・・・・・・・・・・・40-41

Kanreki celebration・・・・・・・・・・・・・・・18-19
   Kanreki celebration・・・・・・・・・・・・・・・38-39

Omeza (wake-up gifts)・・・・・・・・・・・・・・20-21
   Crane petit envelope・・・・・・・・・・・・・・・42-43

Octagonal Tatou・・・・・・・・・・・・・・・・・・・22

Kuromoji case・・・・・・・・・・・・・・・・・・・・23
   Crane case・・・・・・・・・・・・・・・・・・・・52-53

Crane chopstick case・・・・・・・・・・・・・・24-25

Incense envelope・・・・・・・・・・・・・・・・・26-27

Maney envelope・・・・・・・・・・・・・・・・・・・28
   Besic money envelope Ⅰ・・・・・・・・・・・・54-55
   Besic money envelope Ⅱ・・・・・・・・・・・・56-57

Shirt・・・・・・・・・・・・・・・・・・・・・・・・・29
   Shirt package・・・・・・・・・・・・・・・・・・58-59

Celebratory occasions・・・・・・・・・・・・・・30-31

Basic folding techniques・・・・・・・・・・・・・32-33

60

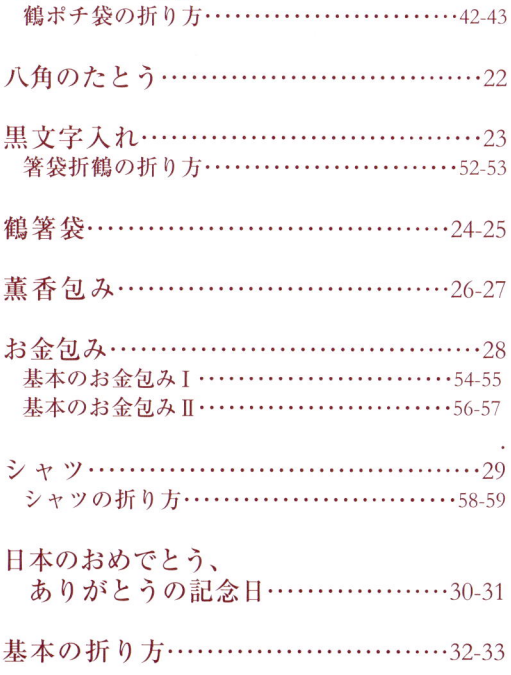

索引

平和を願って鶴を折ります……………2-3
　基本の鶴の折り方………………………34-35

神への供え物を包む……………………4-5
　葉書包みの折り方………………………44-45
　供え物包みの折り方……………………46-47
　略式紙幣包みの折り方…………………48-49

日本人の包む文化………………………7-8
　寿祝儀袋…………………………………36-37

結婚式で使うメッセージカード立て・
　招待状入れ・寸志入れ……………………9

胡麻包み……………………………………10

小物入れの包み……………………………11
　うさぎたとうの折り方…………………50-51

日本の五節句………………………………12

私のひな祭り………………………………13

端午の節句…………………………………17
　兜のポチ袋の折り方……………………40-41

還暦のお祝い……………………………18-19
　還暦祝い袋の折り方……………………38-39

"おめざ"の習慣…………………………20-21
　鶴ポチ袋の折り方………………………42-43

八角のたとう………………………………22

黒文字入れ…………………………………23
　箸袋折鶴の折り方………………………52-53

鶴箸袋……………………………………24-25

薫香包み…………………………………26-27

お金包み……………………………………28
　基本のお金包みⅠ………………………54-55
　基本のお金包みⅡ………………………56-57

シャツ………………………………………29
　シャツの折り方…………………………58-59

日本のおめでとう、
　ありがとうの記念日…………………30-31

基本の折り方……………………………32-33

Afterword

The Great East Japan Earthquake struck Japan on March 11, 2011.
While Japan was filled with great sadness, I watched the television news of children in the foreign countries folding thousand cranes for the Japanese.
Orizuru (Origami cranes) was a form of pray all over the world.

Paper wrapping has long been taught to women at home
as the essential knowledge for their life.
As a play in the childhood and then as manners in everyday life,
the practice has been passed down.

Visible things are changing greatly, and so are values.
I believe that everyone still wants for a secure feeling
that a baby has in mother's womb.

The Japanese is originally taciturn. With few words,
people communicate messages and considerations
in the form of paper wrapping.
The purpose of this book is to convey such practice
to the future generations.

I would like to extend my sincere appreciation to all those
who made possible the publication of this book.

Wishing that the earth would be a beautiful planet forever.

September 17, 2011
Mikico Yokogawa

あとがき

2011年3月11日、日本で、東日本大震災が起こりました。
日本中が悲しみに包まれている中、異国で日本人の為に
千羽鶴を折る子供達をテレビで見ました。
折鶴は世界中の祈りの形になっていました。

紙を折って物を包むことは、古来より日本の女性のたしなみとして
嫁ぐ迄に、家庭で教えられていました。子供の頃は遊びの中で、成長
するに従い日常の中での礼儀作法の形として伝えられました。

目に見える物は大きく変化しています、それに伴って価値観も大きく
変化しています。しかし母の胎内で守られ育てられたときの
安心感を、誰もが求めているのではないでしょうか。

元来日本人は寡黙です。言葉は少なくとも贈り物を紙で包み、
その形で全てを感じ、想いが通じあう、そんな包む形をわずかでも
日本の未来に残したいと願いこの本を作りました。

出版出来ましたことを、心からの感謝を持って
関係各位様に御礼を申し上げます。

地球が永遠に美しい星で在ることを祈っています

2011年9月17日
横川 三希子

編・著者紹介

● **希夢工房** ── Since 1978
　KIMU-KOUBOU
・あなたの希望と夢を形にするデザイン工房です

● **横川三希子** ──1947年東京生まれ
　Mikico Yokogawa
・パッケージデザイン
　公益社団法人 日本パッケージデザイン協会所属
・イラストレーション
・カリグラフ
・セラミックアート
・商業施設、地場産業の企画

● **横川　巧** ──1975年大阪生まれ
　Takumi Yokogawa
・コンストラクション
・パッケージデザイン
・グラフィックデザイン

──── ご協力いただきました ────

（株）有高扇山堂
（株）いづみ企画
香司　鬼頭天薫堂　鎌倉
銀座　香十
（株）サザエ食品
（株）すみの（結納）
NPO法人みのりコミュニオンたんぽぽ
（株）日本香堂
（株）丸廣紙業

アイウエオ順　敬称略

紙材・BOX　　　　前川禎廣
デザインスタッフ　河内直美
写真撮影　　　　　大野　博
翻訳　　　　　　　森田　碧
製作　　　　　　　小野岡廣子

折紙包み　日本の紙遊び

2011年9月17日　初版第1刷発行
2014年9月1日　初版第2刷発行

編・著者　　　　　　　　　　　　希夢工房
企画・デザイン・文　　　　　　　横川三希子
折形コンストラクション・製図・レイアウト　横川 巧
発行者　　　　　　　　　　　　　梶原正弘
発行所　　　　　　株式会社めるくまーる
　　　　　　〒101-0051　東京都千代田区神田神保町1-11
　　　　　　電話 03-3518-2003　URL http://www.merkmal.biz/
印刷・製本　ベクトル印刷株式会社

© 希夢工房（KIMU-KOUBOU）2011
ISBN978-4-8397-0147-5　Printed in Japan

乱丁・落丁本はお取り替えいたします。